I0489654

Survive and Thrive: Sun Tzu's Strategies for Business

Proven tactics
to compete

Eric CYC

Copyright © 2023 Eric CYC

All rights reserved.
ISBN: 9798388664143

PREAMBLE

Since its first publication several centuries ago, The Art of War has been widely recognised as one of the most influential works on military strategy and tactics.

The battlefield is not the only place where we can learn lessons; in fact, they have been successfully implemented in business and industry.

In this new edition of "The Art of War", I have updated each chapter to adapt them to the commercial and industrial context of our time. I have taken care to include concrete and precise examples for each category of activity, whether primary, secondary or tertiary.

The law of three sectors is an economic theory that divides the economy into three sectors of activity: the exploitation and extraction of natural resources (primary), the processing of primary raw materials (secondary), and services (tertiary).

By applying Sun Tzu's teachings to business activities, I hope to help readers become visionary leaders in their respective fields. The tips and strategies presented in this book can help businesses reach new heights of success, while focussing on sustainability and social responsibility.

Whether you are a first-time entrepreneur or a seasoned leader, I hope this guide will help you transform your business and position yourself as a leader in your field.

In the rest of this book, I use a benchmark of the different sectors of the world of work with these fictitious companies:

Primary sector:

Name	Activity	Description
FunCoop	Agriculture	An agricultural cooperative grows 3 types of cereals: wheat, maize and rape
OrAlu	Mining	A company operates an aluminium mine and a gold mine
AtlFish	Fishing	A family business of fishermen exploits fish in the Atlantic
HighSeaCo	Oil exploitation	Company pumps oil and gas on the high seas

Secondary sector:

Name	Activity	Description
DeliFreez	Manufacture of food products	A manufacturer of frozen meals and canned fruit and vegetables
LuxCars	Car manufacturing	A car company makes luxury cars, buses and trucks
PillLab	Pharmaceutical	A laboratory manufactures the medicines that are available over the counter
WoodCo	Building construction	Company builds wooden sheds and houses

Tertiary sector:

Name	Activity	Description
VIPBank	Bank	A private bank manages the portfolios of wealthy people
ColiShip	Transport and Logistics	One company transports parcels for individuals
LearnHub	Education	An educational centre offers courses from 11 years old
WarAid	Charity	Institution offers medical aid in war zones

Table of contents

ACKNOWLEDGEMENTS

I want to express my deepest gratitude to all those who have helped enrich and sharpen my knowledge over the years in pleasant and often rather difficult times.

Among these inspiring people, it is worth mentioning

In the field of banking and finance:

- Lena L., CEO of a private bank, whose experience and strategic vision have been a constant source of inspiration and insight into the issues and challenges of the banking sector. Her actions have been beneficial, so it is justified that she occupies the top spot on the list.

- Evi P., Head of Operational Risk and Data Analysis in the field of finance, who shared her boundless expertise. She helped strengthen the author's skills in this area.

- Lia P., Head of a Mediterranean private bank, with a very fraternal and communicative approach with all people she approaches to spread her knowledge.

In the field of marketing and sales:

- Maxime D., Sales Director in the pharmaceutical industry, for his valuable discussions on managing sales teams and developing effective sales strategies.

- Claire S., Digital Marketing Consultant, who offered her expertise in online marketing and content strategies to help the author better understand current marketing trends.

In the field of engineering and innovation:

- Thomas R., Chief Engineer in the aeronautical industry, for his teachings on the importance of technological innovation and complex project management.

I apologise for the others "left out" of this list, but it was not reasonable to have a long chapter to mention them.

I am excited to continue learning and sharing my knowledge with readers and professionals from all sectors.

Share your opinions, ideas, and knowledge, and stay tuned to hear more. This is essential for improving the safety, performance, and efficiency of a company.

Keep in mind the benefits that flow from this:

- **Enrichment of perspectives**: The experience of diverse employees broadens the horizons and brings in new and innovative ideas. This fosters creativity and adaptability to market challenges and opportunities.

- **Improved decision-making**: The exchange of ideas and knowledge sharing contributes to a better understanding of the issues, which facilitates informed and strategic decision-making.

- **Process optimisation**: The dissemination of experience and skills gained can help identify inefficiencies and flaws in existing processes, thereby improving the productivity and profitability of the company.

- **Strengthening security**: The exchange of information and best practices among employees can help strengthen the security of the company, by identifying and mitigating potential risks.

- **Skills development**: Sharing knowledge and experience encourages continuous training of employees, resulting in a more competent and versatile workforce.

- **Improved employee satisfaction**: A work environment where the exchange of ideas and mutual learning is valued promotes employee development and strengthens their commitment to the company.

- **Increased competitiveness**: By drawing on the diverse experiences and skills of its employees, a company can develop innovative and effective strategies to differentiate itself from its competitors and conquer new markets.

Promoting diversity, the exchange of ideas, and knowledge sharing is crucial, as it not only contributes to improved performance and efficiency, but also to the creation of a strong and dynamic organisational culture.

Thanks to the generosity and sharing of the knowledge of these talented professionals. This guide reflects my solid and versatile expertise developed over time.

1   MARKET AND COMPETITION ASSESSMENT

1) Assess markets and competitors to maximise your chances of success.

The preliminary phase of any business is to maximise your chances of success in the marketplace. If you want to introduce an innovative product or service, it is imperative to understand the needs and expectations of your customers and the competition you will face.

Understand what your customers need, then design your product or service to meet those needs. Ensure sure your offering is truly unique and valuable.

This will allow you to position yourself effectively in the market and differentiate yourself from your real competitors.

To assess the market objectively, you should look at trends, statistics, and the preferences of your target audience. Naturally, you must keep up to date with the latest industry developments, new technologies, and changes in consumer preferences and requirements.

Additionally, to understand your competitors' strengths and weaknesses, you must carefully observe their activities. This will help you seize opportunities to differentiate yourself from the competition and develop strategies to outperform them.

Assessing the market and competition is a continuous and regular task. It is unthinkable to do it once and then ignore changes in the market. You need to be constantly aware of industry developments and new trends.

This will help you to be better prepared to deal with changing market conditions and to maintain your competitive edge.

2) Use demographics and trends to assess client needs

The use of demographic data is a strategic lever for designing products and services that meet specific customer needs. The same applies to anticipating future trends and positioning oneself competitively in the market.

As a first step, the collection of demographic data is essential to capture the profiles of its current and potential customers. This data can include information such as age, gender, occupation, income, and interests, etc. Rigorously analyse this data and use it to gain a comprehensive understanding of customers' needs and preferences.

Second, the company should endeavour to study current and future trends in the industry. This analysis will provide insight into market movements, emerging needs, and future trends. By incorporating these trends into the company's strategy, the company will be able to differentiate itself from the competition and successfully position itself in the market.

Demographic data can help identify market opportunities disregarded until now. In this way, a company can discover under-exploited market segments, which can enable it to develop new products and services tailored to the needs of these specific segments.

Primary sector:

Name	Objective : To assess the needs of customers in terms of ...	Method : Collecting demographic data to understand ...
FunCoop	Agricultural products	food habits and consumer preferences
OrAlu	Precious metals	current and future demand for precious metals and aluminium
AtlFish	Fresh fish	consumer preferences for fish and seafood
HighSeaCo	Oil and gas products	consumer preferences in terms of energy and fuel

Secondary sector:

Name	Objective : To propose suitable products, understand the trends ...	Method : Collect data on (1) dietary habits and preferences (2) current and future trends in the ...
DeliFreez	Food and consumer preferences	(1) analysis of current and future food trends
LuxCars	Current and future of the automotive market	(2) of the automotive market, analysis of consumer preferences for vehicles
PillLab	Current and future of the pharmaceutical market	(2) of the pharmaceutical market, analysis of consumer preferences for non-prescription medicines
WoodCo	Current and future of construction	(2) of the construction market, analysis of consumer preferences for wooden houses and sheds

Tertiary sector:

Name	Objective:	Method : Analyse demographic data to determine the ...
VIPBank	Understanding the financial needs and goals of high net-worth clients.	Evaluate clients' profiles and financial needs. Propose personalised services and products to meet their demands.
ColiShip	Assess delivery trends and preferences to improve delivery of services.	Current and future demand for precious metals and aluminium

LearnHub	Understanding educational trends and needs to improve educational programme.	Consumer preferences for fish and seafood
WarAid	Understanding health trends and needs in conflict areas.	Consumer preferences in terms of energy and fuel

3) **Assess the competition to determine weaknesses and opportunities.**

Understanding competitors' products and services, prices, positioning, market share and reputation is essential to assessing the competition. Companies need to be aware of their own company's strengths and weaknesses, as well as opportunities for growth, to better design their environment.

Name of the company	Competition problem	Solution 1	Solution 2
FunCoop	Low crop yields	Soil improvement	Use of high-performance seeds
	Competition from large retailers	Development of short supply chains	Crop diversification
OrAlu	High extraction costs	Automation of operations	Use of more efficient equipment
	Deterioration of the environmental image	Adoption of site-rehabilitation techniques	Use of alternative materials
AtlFish	Decreases in fish stocks	Use of more sustainable fishing techniques	Search for new fishing grounds
	Competition from imports	Promotion of local products	Diversification of products offered
HighSeaCo	Falling oil prices	Reduction in extraction costs	Search for new deposits
	High environmental costs	Adoption of cleaner technologies	Development of alternative energy sources

Name of the company	Competition problem	Solution 1	Solution 2
DeliFreez	Product differentiation	Creation of new exclusive products	Investment in advertising and marketing to raise awareness
	High production costs	Optimisation of production costs	Search for new suppliers of raw materials
LuxCars	Pressure from foreign competition	Research and development to improve performance and quality	Reduction of production costs
	Compliance with environmental regulations	Use of recyclable materials	Investment in more environmentally friendly technologies
PillLab	Pressure from generics	Development of new innovative products	Aggressive pricing strategy to counter the competition
	High research and development costs	Reduction of production costs	Collaboration with other companies to share research and development costs
WoodCo	Competition from foreign companies	Differentiation through product quality	Improving employee training and expertise
	Pressure on prices	Reduction in production costs	Emphasis on quality and after-sales service
VIPBank	Competition from large banks	Offering personalised advisory and investment services for high net-worth clients.	Set up loyalty programmes for regular customers.
	Cybersecurity issues	Implement robust security protocols to protect customer information.	Use IT security experts to monitor and detect any suspicious activity.
ColiShip	Competitors offering lower rates	Improve supply chain efficiency to reduce costs.	Offer faster and more reliable transport services to differentiate from competitors.
	Lack of flexibility in delivery options	Offer flexible delivery options, such as evening and weekend deliveries.	Allow customers to choose the time and place of delivery for greater convenience.

Name of the company	Competition problem	Solution 1	Solution 2
LearnHub	Competition from institutions offering online programmes	Investing in innovative educational technologies to provide a high-quality e-learning experience.	Provide courses that involve practical application.
	Funding problems	Offer grants and loans to students in financial need.	Seek partnerships with companies to fund relevant educational programmes.
WarAid	Competition with other charities	Offer innovative and personalised support programmes for people in need.	Collaborate with other organisations to maximise impact.
	Difficulty in raising funds	Use social media to raise awareness of the cause and collect donations online.	Organise fundraising events to involve the local community.

4) **Use analytical tools such as SWOT and PESTEL to assess your business and market**

Definition of SWOT:

SWOT is an acronym that stands for Strengths, Weaknesses, Opportunities, and Threats. SWOT is a strategic analysis tool used to assess the competitive position of a company in its market. It identifies the internal and external factors that can affect the company's performance.

Strengths are the internal advantages that the company has over the competition. Weaknesses are the internal disadvantages that the company must overcome to improve its competitive position.

Opportunities are the external factors that the company can exploit to improve its performance. Threats are those external factors that can negatively affect the company's performance.

By using SWOT, companies can identify areas where they must focus their efforts to improve their competitive position. This can help companies define strategies to differentiate themselves from the competition, improve their product or service offering, and prepare for future changes in the market.

Anyone can use SWOT to assess their industry, regardless of the size and scope of their company - from start-ups to multinationals. The company may use this internally to evaluate its position, and analysts outside the company can employ it to examine a company's place in the market.

Some SWOT software is available on the market:

- Creately: an online software that allows you to create SWOT and other types of diagrams.

- SWOT Analysis App: a mobile application for iOS devices that makes it easy to create and share SWOT analyses.

- Gliffy: another online software that allows you to create SWOT charts, as well as other types of charts.

- MindView: mind mapping software that includes features for creating SWOT analyses.

- SmartDraw: a diagramming software that provides templates for SWOT and other types of analysis.

- SWOT Analysis Software: a software specifically dedicated to the creation of SWOT analyses.

Definition of PESTEL :

PESTEL is an acronym that stands for Political, Economic, Societal, Technological, Environmental, and Legal. PESTEL is an environmental analysis tool used to assess the economic factors that can affect a company's performance.

Each letter in PESTEL represents a category of analysis:

Political: Political factors include regulations, government policies, and laws that may affect the business.

Economic: Economic factors include overall economic conditions such as inflation, economic growth, and interest rates.

Societal: Societal factors include social trends and attitudes such as lifestyles, values, consumer behaviour, etc.

Technological: Technological factors include technological developments and advances that may affect the business.

Environmental: Environmental factors include environmental considerations such as climate change, sustainability, waste management, etc.

Legal: Legal factors include laws and regulations that may affect the business.

Thanks to PESTEL, companies can determine precisely which external factors can strongly influence their success. This analysis allows them to identify the real opportunities and risks in their environment and to adapt their strategy to meet the circumstances.

The PESTEL framework applies perfectly to all business areas and companies, from newcomers to multinationals. Analysts use it to review a company's internal environment or the broad industry externally.

Here are some examples of PESTEL software available:

- PESTLE Analysis Template: An easy-to-use Excel template that allows you to track the political, economic, social, technological, environmental and legal factors that affect your business.

- Miro: an online collaboration tool that includes a PESTEL model to help teams assess environmental trends and influence their business.

- StratNavApp: a strategic planning platform that uses PESTEL analysis to help companies assess their business environment.

- MindManager: mind mapping software that includes PESTEL models to help teams assess the external factors affecting their business.

- Asana: a complete online solution from process generation to project management with interesting solutions.

5) Adapt your strategy according to the continuous evaluation of your market

The proposed strategies are based on:

- Adapting to new market trends

- Research and innovation to improve business efficiency

- Diversification to respond to new markets or to prevent the risks associated with dependence on a single activity.

Name	Strategy
FunCoop	<ul><li>Diversify crop types to avoid dependence on a single crop.</li><li>Innovate by using more environmentally friendly production methods to meet the expectations of environmentally conscious consumers.</li><li>Increase the efficiency of the production chain to reduce costs and increase competitiveness.</li></ul>
OrAlu	<ul><li>Increase market share by producing more aluminium and developing the production of aluminium products.</li><li>Diversify activities by investing in the mining of other metals.</li><li>Improve the efficiency of the production line by optimising processes to reduce costs.</li></ul>
AtlFish	<ul><li>Invest in research and development to improve product quality and meet market demands.</li><li>Establish partnerships with local companies to ensure rapid distribution and better accessibility of products.</li><li>Diversify activities by investing in aquaculture to offer different products and better meet consumer expectations.</li></ul>
HighSeaCo	<ul><li>Diversify activities by investing in renewable energy production to meet environmental requirements.</li><li>Adopt modern technologies to improve the efficiency of the production line.</li><li>Develop a policy of social responsibility to meet consumer expectations and improve the company's reputation.</li></ul>
DeliFreez	<ul><li>Offer a more varied range of products to meet the growing consumer demand for healthy and organic food</li><li>Use more advanced technologies to improve production efficiency and reduce costs</li><li>Focus on expanding online sales to reach a wider audience</li></ul>
LuxCars	<ul><li>Develop new electric car models to meet the growing consumer need for environmentally friendly cars</li><li>Establish partnerships with other companies to offer additional services such as car maintenance and repair</li><li>Provide promotional offers to build customer loyalty and encourage sales</li></ul>

Name	Strategy
PillLab	<ul><li>Expanding the product range to meet the growing consumer need for natural and alternative medicines</li><li>Set up targeted marketing campaigns to reach a wider audience</li><li>Partner with health organisations to increase brand visibility</li></ul>
WoodCo	<ul><li>Invest in the research and development of new materials to improve product quality</li><li>Expanding the product range to meet the growing consumer need for environmentally friendly products</li><li>Adopt sustainable production practices to meet increasing customer demands for environmental responsibility.</li></ul>
VIPBank	<ul><li>Improve the customer experience by offering personalised online services</li><li>Offer competitive interest rates</li><li>Expanding the range of products and services offered</li></ul>
ColiShip	<ul><li>Investing in technology to improve parcel management</li><li>Offer flexible and fast delivery options</li><li>Develop loyalty programmes for regular customers</li></ul>
LearnHub	<ul><li>Developing online courses to meet the needs of international students</li><li>Expanding course offerings to include specialist subjects</li><li>Establishing partnerships with renowned universities</li></ul>
WarAid	<ul><li>Develop partnerships with other organisations to maximise the impact</li><li>Improve fundraising using online platforms and social networks</li><li>Using demographic data to better understand the needs of war-affected communities</li></ul>

2   STRATEGIC PLANNING AND ANTICIPATION

1) Plan for the long term to achieve your goals.

Companies need to be forward-looking and take the time to plan for the long term to maximise their profitability, competitiveness, sustainability and customer satisfaction. They must also be willing to adjust their strategy accordingly to achieve their longer-term goals.

The success of a business depends on long-term planning. Anticipating changes in the economic environment and defining long-term objectives should be possible. By working together on this planning, we can develop a clear vision of the company's future and outline strategies to reach its goals.

By planning for the long term, you can make informed decisions that maximise benefits. Ensure transparent and understandable communication of the company's long-term vision at all levels. This helps to align the company's activities with its long-term strategy, which contributes to greater organisational productivity and efficiency.

Although they can be challenging, economic trends and forecasts need to be analysed. This requires a careful assessment of the company's resources and its ability to achieve its objectives. A thorough analysis of the market and economic environment and a good understanding of the company's activities and objectives are necessary for effective strategic planning.

Companies that do not plan for long-term risk miss opportunities and fail to prepare adequately for sudden changes. Do not consider it as a static process. The company must ensure that they adequately factor in any changes in the economic environment and their objectives. To adapt to multiple changes over time, it must remain flexible.

2) Develop contingency plans to deal with unforeseen situations

In the event of equipment problems, service interruptions, or emergencies, companies must be prepared to act quickly and develop plans to limit the impact of unexpected events on their business.

The cost of these plans is an insurance investment worth considering.

In all sectors, the actions needed to manage the unexpected are:

- **- Risk identification**: conduct a thorough risk assessment for each sector of activity and for each individual company. This identification should consider all possible scenarios to develop contingency plans for each situation.

- **- Develop effective communication strategies**: Have communication plans in place to disseminate information to employees, customers and all stakeholders in the event of an unexpected situation. These plans should be clear, detailed and easily accessible to ensure quick and effective communication.

- **- Develop training programmes**: Regularly train employees on emergency procedures and contingency plans. Tailor this training to each hierarchical level of the company so that employees can be aware of their roles and responsibilities when an unanticipated scenario arises.

- **- Evaluate contingency plans**: test contingency plans regularly to ensure their effectiveness. Organisers should plan and organise tests to simulate real-life situations.

- **- Ensure data integrity by implementing regular back-up measures**: Implement back-up systems to ensure business continuity in the event of a disaster or computer failure. These backup systems should be regularly tested and updated.

- **- Work in synergy with external collaborators**: Work closely with partners to ensure business continuity. Contingency plans should consider relationships with partners, suppliers, and customers. Contingency plans should be prepared to ensure that business could continue in the event of an unforeseen situation.

Additionally, for our list of companies, more precisely, we can add among others:

Company	Contingency plans
FunCoop	• Establish a contingency plan for natural disasters or animal disease outbreaks. • Establish partnerships to exchange resources when needed. • Train cooperative members on how to minimise losses.
OrAlu	• Establish an emergency plan for mining accidents and environmental problems, such as chemical leaks. • Maintain strong relationships with local communities to facilitate a rapid response in times of need. • Train staff on mine explosion safety measures
AtlFish	• Establish management for environmental issues, such as oil spills or climate change. • Maintain relationships with local fishermen to ensure supply • Establish monitoring systems to detect health problems in fish and other marine creatures.
HighSeaCo	• Establish a plan for responding to emergencies at sea, such as storms or engine failures. • Maintain relationships with fuel suppliers to ensure a continuous supply. • Teach the crew safety measures and procedures to follow in case of an emergency.
DeliFreez	• Sufficient storage of raw materials to cope with increased demand; • Implementation of a quality management system to prevent food safety problems; • Have a reliable and efficient transport network to deliver products to customers.
LuxCars	• Have a regular preventive maintenance system to ensure the proper functioning of vehicles; • Have a spare parts stock management system to be able to replace defective parts quickly; • Implement a regular training programme for drivers to raise their awareness of road safety.

Company	Contingency plans
PillLab	• Establish a crisis management team to deal with emergencies; • Establish a contingency plan for business continuity in the event of natural disasters or other unforeseen events; • Have a security system to protect sensitive data and information.
WoodCo	• Have a sufficient stock of raw materials to avoid production interruptions; • Implement a quality monitoring system to ensure the quality of finished products; • Have a contingency plan to deal with forest fires and other natural disasters that may affect operations.
VIPBank	• Establish a clear communication plan to inform customers in the event of a service interruption. • Identify key staff who need to be able to work remotely in an emergency. • Develop a physical security plan for agencies in the event of a natural disaster or national emergency.
ColiShip	• Establish a communication plan to inform customers of delays or interruptions in service. • Establish a list of alternative suppliers to ensure continuity of supply in the event of a crisis. • Implement a stock management system to ensure that key products are always available.
LearnHub	• Establish a clear communication plan to inform students in the event of a disruption to classes. • Identify key teachers who can work remotely in an emergency. • Develop a physical security plan for campuses in the event of a natural disaster or national emergency.
WarAid	• Establish a communication plan to inform service beneficiaries in the event of a service interruption or change. • Identify key aid workers who need to be able to work remotely in an emergency. • Establish partnerships with other organisations to ensure continuity of service in the event of a crisis.

3) Using scenario analysis to anticipate future market changes

This method forecasts future market changes by considering economic, political, social and environmental factors and making assumptions. By using this method, companies can develop action plans in the event of significant changes, thereby reducing the risk of significant losses.

A company in the industry can prepare for rising raw material costs by looking for cheaper alternatives and negotiating long-term contracts.

Business in the commercial service sector can plan promotional offers or discounts to retain its customers in the event of a decline in the purchasing power of its customers.

Scenario analysis enables companies to make informed decisions, considering future risks and opportunities. In this way, they can fully maintain their advantage in a changing market.

4) Develop an action plan that incorporates the results of your market assessment

To succeed in a competitive market, it is necessary to develop an effective strategy. Fully understanding the desired outcomes and the necessary steps to achieve them is essential for success.

Based on the results of a market assessment, companies can adapt to changes in the market and consumer demand, and thus improve their products and services to become more competitive.

We will look at how to develop a customised action plan for each company, considering its objectives, market and competitors.

Company	Action plans
FunCoop	• Analyse market trends to anticipate future developments and new customer needs. • Adapting agricultural practices to meet environmental and societal concerns. • Focus on high value-added products to improve profitability.
OrAlu	• Diversify activities to reduce dependence on a single product or market. • Identify new markets for existing products to expand the customer base. • Invest in research and development to improve extraction efficiency and reduce costs.
AtlFish	• Adopt sustainable fishing practices to ensure the preservation of marine resources. • Set up agreements with distributors to increase the visibility of products and reach a wider customer base. • Develop new products from non-marketed fish to minimise waste and improve profitability.
HighSeaCo	• Collect data on customer buying habits, market trends and technological innovations. • Set clear objectives for your action plan. Objectives should be specific, measurable, achievable, relevant and time-bound. The company might set a goal of increasing its market share by 10% over the next year. • The people responsible for implementing specific actions, including the time frame and resources needed, should do so within the next few days. To increase market share, this should include developing new products or services, increasing production capacity, or improving customer service.
DeliFreez	• Regularly assess market trends and consumer tastes to adapt the range of products offered. • Work closely with suppliers to ensure a stable and reliable supply chain. • Create partnerships with restaurants and food shops to diversify distribution channels.
LuxCars	• Conduct regular competitive analysis to adapt to market trends and provide benefit to customers. • Set up loyalty programmes to encourage customers to return and recommend the company to others. • By investing in technologies, companies can increase the quality of the vehicles they produce and decrease production costs.

Company	Action plans
PillLab	<ul><li>Develop contingency plans to deal with unforeseen situations such as raw material shortages or production interruptions.</li><li>Implementing strict quality controls to ensure the safety and efficacy of the medicines produced.</li><li>Establish partnerships with universities and research laboratories to remain at the forefront of scientific and technological advances.</li></ul>
WoodCo	<ul><li>Plan sustainable resource management to ensure a sustainable and environmentally friendly supply chain.</li><li>Innovate in the design of new products to meet customer expectations and improve the company's profitability.</li><li>Establish partnerships with construction companies to ensure the optimal use of manufactured products and long-term growth.</li></ul>
VIPBank	<ul><li>Use market data to identify customer needs and adapt services accordingly.</li><li>Integrate the results of the evaluation into the overall marketing strategy, using the most effective communication channels to reach the target customers.</li><li>Implement a process of continuous monitoring of market developments, to adjust strategies and action plans according to customer demands.</li></ul>
ColiShip	<ul><li>Use market data to optimise logistics and improve operational efficiency.</li><li>Develop a communication plan that incorporates the results of the market assessment, focussing on the company's competitive advantages.</li><li>Establish a contingency plan to deal with unforeseen situations such as market fluctuations, transport problems, etc.</li></ul>
LearnHub	<ul><li>Adapting learning programmes in line with market trends and customer needs.</li><li>Develop a communication plan that uses the results of the evaluation to promote the benefits of the training programmes and attract new clients.</li><li>Establish an action plan to improve the user experience, using customer comments and feedback to optimise the features and services offered.</li></ul>
WarAid	<ul><li>Use market data to identify the areas most at risk and adjust action plans accordingly.</li><li>Develop a communication plan that incorporates the results of the market assessment, highlighting the organization's expertise and effectiveness in emergencies.</li><li>Establish a system for continuous monitoring of global trends and events, to adapt quickly to unforeseen situations and to respond to the needs of communities affected by crises.</li></ul>

5) Using economic and political forecasts to prepare your business for change

Economic forecasts and changes are crucial in predicting changes in exchange rates, interest rates, consumer habits and regulations that will affect your business. Additionally, political forecasting can be crucial in anticipating binding tax changes that will affect your business performance.

For your business to be effective, you must conduct a rigorous analysis of economic and political trends and indicators before utilising economic and political forecasts. Sources such as government agencies, central banks, research companies and consultancies can provide data.

Using this data, you will be able to identify trends relevant to your company and plan accordingly. Given the negative economic forecasts for your sector, assess potential cost-cutting or diversification strategies to reduce the risks.

Similarly, if the policy forecast reveals a change that could affect your business, you can plan adaptive measures such as product adjustment, licencing or strategic reorientation.

Whatever the sector, to use economic and political forecasts to prepare your business for change, the basic tips are:

- **- Keep up to date with economic and political news**: stay informed about current and future economic and political trends to better anticipate changes and adjust strategy accordingly.

- **- Establish sustainable partnerships**: Working with reliable and strong partners can help reduce the risks associated with economic and political change. Select partners who have a real understanding of economic and political trends and who can adapt quickly to changes. Without entering politics, be neutral in your contact with all.

- **- Be versatile**: diversification of activities can help reduce the company's exposure to economic and political risks. Economic or political changes can affect one activity, but other activities can still create income.

- **- Keep a legal watch to ensure compliance with regulations**: regulatory changes can have a significant impact on businesses. Monitor regulatory developments and adapt in a timely manner.

- **- Establish a contingency plan**: this type of event should be included in a contingency plan.

6) Using strategic planning to align your business goals with your resources

Strategic planning remains a key process for companies seeking to align their objectives with their resources. It helps to define a clear vision for the business, determine the means to achieve the goals, prioritise initiatives and pursue their implementation.

This process assists in accurately pinpointing the company's advantages, drawbacks, opportunities and threats as well as possible risks and means to reduce them.

Here are some of the best tips that apply to all businesses:

- **Be obvious, about what you want to complete** setting a clear vision for the company helps focus on long-term goals and align actions with the overall strategy.

- **Assess market growth potential**: analyse the market, trends and customers should identify potential opportunities and threats to the business.

- **Evaluate internal performance to improve operational efficiency**: to maximise efficiency, identify strengths and weaknesses to highlight strengths and correct weaknesses.

- **Define SMART objectives**: objectives must be specific, measurable, achievable, relevant and time-bound to be effective in strategic planning.

- **Develop action plans in consideration of the objectives to reach:** create action plans for each strategic objective that specify the steps to take, deadlines, resources required and people responsible for performing those plans.

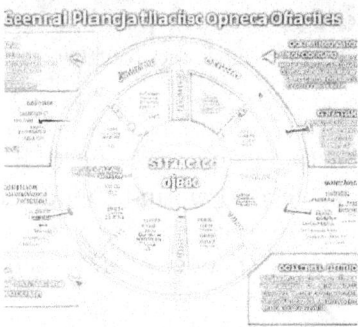

3   OFFENSIVE MARKETING STRATEGIES

1) Using advertising to reach potential customers

Advertising is an excellent way for companies to reach deep into potential customers and to promote effectively their products and services. It provides wide visibility and brand awareness, a clear advantage for any type of business.

Here are some tips on how to use advertising effectively:

- **Tailor the message to reach the target audience**: to make your advertising campaign successful, carefully analyse the profile and interests of your target audience. We recommend that you assess their buying habits and understand their needs so that your promotional messages are in line with their demands.

- **Use an empathetic approach when communicating**: creativity and originality are essential to capture consumers' attention. Include bright colours, images and strong messages in your advertising to captivate and quickly communicate your message.

- **Determine the appropriate distribution channels**: to optimise your communication and reach your target audience, you must select the appropriate distribution channels: magazines, newspapers, TV or radio spots, billboards, online media and social networks. In this way, you maximise the reach and effectiveness of your marketing message for your company.

- **Incorporate testimonials and reviews into your communication strategy**: customer testimonials and reviews can be very effective tools in advertising. Satisfied customers can help convince new customers by sharing their positive experience with your company. Use testimonials and reviews in your advertising to build credibility for your business.

- **Harness the power of humour to engage and maintain the interest of your target audience**: humour is a powerful and effective way to capture the attention of consumers. By incorporating humour into your advertising, you provide users with entertaining content that can be shared on social networks and spread widely, which is beneficial for promoting your business to a wider audience.

- **Focus on sincere and constructive interactions based on mutual respect**: customers seek authenticity and honesty, so we encourage you to ensure that your company's advertising is clear and transparent. By avoiding false promises or misleading messages, you will build customer trust in your company and contribute to its positive reputation.

To illustrate these successful advertising approaches, consider the following:

- "Dumb Ways to DieMetro Trains' "Dumb Ways to Die": the dark humour made this ad stand out and catch the attention of young people, providing an entertaining way to convey the key message of rail safety. Growing popularity in social media has led to a popular mobile game based on the ad campaign.

- "Petit Bateau" in 2018, the Petit Bateau brand managed to reach a wider audience by selecting adults and highlighting their clothing. This approach allowed consumers to identify a nostalgic feeling of childhood, granting a sense of well-being and comfort. Owing to this effective example of message adaptation, the advertisement proved extremely popular.

- Old Spice's "The Man Your Man Could Smell Like" creates a sense of empathy with men by emphasising that confidence and a noble appearance are affordable through its products. It combines humour and satire to show men how they can be more attractive to women, providing a concrete example of empathetic communication. In addition, she encourages individuals to develop their confidence so that they can feel better about themselves.

- "Les Fruits et Légumes Moches" by Intermarché. This moving ad illustrates an empathetic approach to communication. By highlighting fruit and vegetables that are imperfect in appearance, it emphasises that they nevertheless retain their taste and nutritional qualities intact. Furthermore, the personification of the products through voices and facial expressions makes it possible to affect the consumer sensitively while encouraging them to respect and appreciate "ugly" foods.

- Coca-Cola's "Share a Coke" campaign. The company implemented a campaign to personalise Coca-Cola bottles with popular names to encourage consumers to buy products bearing their first name or that of a close friend. To ensure mass and effective distribution, the company chose several channels, including television, radio, social media and print advertising.

- "The Moldy Whopper" by Burger King. In 2020, the team posted a video on YouTube and various social networks. The video illustrated Burger King's commitment to fresh products with no artificial preservatives and showed the natural moulding process of a Burger King Whopper.

- "Real Beauty Sketches" by Dove, released in 2013. Women in this advert are asked to provide an artist with a description of their own appearance even though the artist cannot see them, and other women will do the same. The resulting drawings revealed that as well as being extremely critical of themselves, others tended to perceive the beauty of these women differently and often with more positivity. The public praised the advert for its capacity to evoke strong emotions and its faithful representation of the experiences of these women.

- "Ultrasound"from Doritos: During an ultrasound, this couple discovers that the baby reacts surprisingly when the father-to-be eats a Dorito. The resulting comical scene entertains viewers with the Doritos crisp advertisement.

- "The Spies" for the film Kingsman: This promotional ad parodies the spy genre by exploiting humour. The amusing tone immediately grabs the attention of the various viewers and encourages them to watch the film.

- "Like a Girl" by Always. This advert features girls of different ages playing sports or engaged in various activities. It illustrates how the suggestion to "do things like a girl" can sometimes project a negative and discriminatory message. This content has proven to be very remarkable, as it works to encourage dialogue around gender issues and builds a positive sense of self-esteem in young women. With its inherent frankness and respect, this advert raises awareness of the importance of promoting rather than degrading women.

2) Using social networks to establish an online presence and reach a wider audience

Your company can easily tap into the potential of social networks, regardless of where it is in the production chain. To achieve this, you will need to identify the best social network for your target audience and understand more about where their most active points are.

In particular, if your business is targeting a young audience, experts recommend having a presence on Instagram and TikTok. LinkedIn is more suitable for targeting businesses, whereas Facebook may be more effective in reaching consumers.

To retain your audience, you should engage them by providing them with relevant and interesting content. Provide regular updates in the form of videos, photos, blog posts or stories, and interact with your audience by responding to their comments and private messages.

Another important tip is to work with influencers or brand ambassadors. Influencers have a loyal and committed community that can be extremely valuable to your business. By working with influencers, you can target their audience and gain credibility.

It is essential to assess the reach of your social media presence. Look at engagement, followers and conversions to see what is working and what needs to be improved. This will allow you to adjust your strategy and achieve better results.

3) Using content marketing to provide value to potential customers

Content marketing is about generating informative, educational or entertaining content to engage and inform potential customers. Content can be in the form of blogs, videos, infographics, e-books, newsletters, etc.

Content marketing provides potential customers with information that encourages them to take actions that lead to the acquisition.

Here are some tips for using content marketing effectively:

- **Accurately assess the expectations of potential customers**: use keyword research tools to identify the search terms your audience uses to find information about your industry.

- **Develop an effective and consistent publishing timetable**: plan your content in advance by creating a content calendar. This ensures that you are publishing content regularly and that you cover all the key topics for your target audience.

- **Diversify the types of media through which to communicate to reach a wider audience**: to reach a wider audience, it is important to offer various content: videos, infographics, blogs, white papers, case studies and webinars are all formats to consider getting people to consume your content.

- **Use an effective language approach to create engaging and relevant content**: quality content is essential to engage potential customers and get them to act. Create informative, useful and compelling content that meets the needs of your potential customers and encourages them to learn more about your products or services.

- **Optimise the distribution of your content**: content creation is only part of the equation. You also must promote your content to reach a wider audience. Use social media, newsletters, email marketing and paid advertising to promote your content and drive more traffic to your website.

Concrete examples for our core businesses:

- **FunCoop**: create a blog with regular posts about the products the company offers, their benefits and uses. Produce video tutorials to tell customers how to use some of its products. Organise online events such as webinars to share tips and tricks with its community.

- **OrAlu**: improve its communication by creating a series of videos showing the different types of metal it works with and their manufacturing processes. Provide a free how-to guide to help customers choose the right material for their project. Publish case studies on its website to demonstrate how OrAlu has helped customers solve similar problems.

- **AtlFish**: leverage digital media to highlight its products. Create a blog covering the different fish and seafood it offers, as well as recipes for preparing them. Additionally, organise virtual events such as tastings to highlight its products to customers. Simultaneously, use social networks to share images and videos about the products and its fishing process.

- **HighSeaCo**: establish a loyalty programme to reward customers and motivate them to purchase more often. Organise physical events to allow consumers to meet the HighSeaCo team and test its products. Finally, collaborate with local businesses to organise joint events and reach more people.

- **DeliFreez**: Promote its products by creating a series of videos that demonstrate different uses of daily recipes. Organise on-site tastings so that customers can taste their products before making a purchase. Offer discounts and free samples to customers who share their opinions on social networks.

- **LuxCars**: create a series of videos on the latest luxury car trends and the different models available. Hold in-person events to allow customers to see the cars in action and talk to LuxCars experts. Offer-free test-drives to potential customers so they can experience the cars before they buy.

- **PillLab**: create a series of videos about the different types of medicines it offers and the effects they have on the body. Hold in-person events where customers can talk to PillLab pharmacists and ask questions about their medicines. Offer discounts or free samples to customers who share their opinions on social media.

- **WoodCo**: create tutorials to show customers how to do some of the work themselves, highlighting the materials WoodCo offers. Offer virtual tours of their projects, with supporting images and videos. Encourage customers to share their own building and renovation projects on social media, using a company-specific hashtag.

- **VIPBank**: provide value to potential customers by offering blog posts on money management, investments and ways to save money. Create educational videos on different forms of loans, interest rates, and financing options to help customers make informed decisions. Present white papers on complex financial topics such as taxation or wealth management to build credibility as a financial expert.

- **ColiShip**: comfort customers by creating content that helps them understand the different delivery options and forms of transport they can use. Provide guides to international shipping regulations and necessary customs documents. Provide case studies of how it has helped its customers solve complex logistics problems.

- **LearnHub**: offer educational blogs on current topics such as new learning methods, curriculum changes or the latest trends in online education to enhance the value of your potential customers. Provide guides to the different training options available, and run free webinars to help students fully understand their course content.

- **WarAid**: give value to its potential clients by developing content that tells stories of people who have benefited from its programme. Provide blogs on the various types of projects it supports, as well as frequent updates on the results of these projects. Organise webinars to educate people about the challenges they face and how everyone can work together to bring about change.

4) Using the benefits of online advertising to target specific audiences

Whether you represent a small local business or a large international company, online advertising can help you increase your visibility, attract new customers and increase your sales.

Clearly, defining your target audience and designing ads that engage them is crucial to successful online advertising.

By using the targeting tools available on online advertising platforms, you can effectively reach your target audience and maximise your chances of success.

Examples of brands that have successfully used online advertising to reach their target audience:

1. **Coca-Cola**: By using targeted Facebook ads, Coca-Cola could reach specific audiences around the world based on their age, gender, location and interests. By offering personalised content, Coca-Cola was able to engage consumers and create an emotional connection with them.

2. **Amazon**: By exploiting the potential of Google AdWords ads, Amazon was able to reach consumers who were searching for specific products on the web. These ads placed at the top of the results page allowed Amazon to capture the attention of users who wanted to buy what they offered.

3. **Nike**: By targeting Instagram ads specifically to their target audience, Nike successfully reached consumers who are passionate about sports and fitness. With a dynamic selection of images and videos, Nike drove consumer engagement and increased their brand awareness.

4. **Uber**: By implementing targeted YouTube ads, Uber could reach consumers who were looking for a convenient and economical way to get around. With fun and compelling ads, Uber was able to capture customers' attention and amplify its brand visibility.

5) Use marketing techniques such as influencer marketing and native advertising to reach a wider audience

Advertising has become so pervasive that it is becoming increasingly challenging for companies to make a lasting impression on potential customers. Therefore, companies are looking at innovative ways to reach a wider audience. Influencer marketing and native advertising are two marketing techniques that have proven effective in achieving this goal.

Influencer marketing involves working with influencers in a particular field to promote your brand or products. Advertisers use native advertising to blend their messages with the content of a page or media outlet. This type of ad seamlessly integrates into the existing content, providing readers with useful ads and relevant to them.

Known examples of companies that have used these marketing techniques successfully:

1. **L'Oreal Paris**: collaborated with several beauty influencers to promote its new range of hair products. The influencers shared their results with their followers on Instagram, generating visibility for the brand and engaging consumers.

2. **IKEA**: used native advertising to promote its new range of eco-friendly furniture. The brand created a series of educational videos on sustainability, subtly integrating its new products into the content. Home décor sites posted these videos, targeting people interested in the topic.

3. **Volkswagen**: used automotive influencers to help spread the word about its new electric car. They presented their honest opinions and posted photographs of the vehicle on their digital platforms, encouraging consumers to learn more about the product.

4. **Spotify** has implemented an innovative communication strategy to promote personalised music playlists. By integrating ads directly into users' music streams, we introduce them to new playlists and encourage usage.

6) Achieving your business objectives through an effective marketing strategy

The objective of any business is to generate profits by selling its products or services. Marketing strategy can include various techniques such as advertising, promotions, communication, distribution, pricing and market segmentation.

This marketing strategy should be consistent and adapted to changes in the market. To optimise your strategy, be sure to monitor your company's performance and examine your customers' reactions. This will help you adapt to your approach.

Many companies have employed successful marketing strategies to reach their business goals, including:

1) **Apple**: a company known for its innovative marketing strategy, including the release of new products and the use of creative and engaging advertising. Apple has also created an ecosystem of interconnected products that encourages customers to remain loyal to the brand.

2) **Coca-Cola**: For more than a century, Coca-Cola has established itself as a leading brand through its innovative and dynamic advertising campaigns. Additionally, the company has applied market segmentation to address specific messages to different consumer groups.

3) **BMW**: thanks to a well-thought-out communication strategy, BMW has succeeded in distinguishing itself from its competitors by placing its top-of-the-range vehicles in the European market and in building customer loyalty through the impeccable quality of its after-sales service.

4) **H&M**: a fashion company that has managed to maintain its relevance in a competitive market by using an innovative marketing strategy, engaging influencers and collaborating with designers to create excitement around the brand.

5) **Samsung**: The company strategically distinguished itself from competitors in the smartphone sector by emphasising its differences. It does this by using TV ads, promotional events and viral advertising campaigns to promote its products.

6) **Toyota**: The company has focused on the quality and reliability of its cars to form its marketing strategy, and has conducted market segmentation to target various consumer groups with offers tailored to their needs.

4   OPTIMISATION AND RETENTION TACTICS

1) Using data analysis to identify market trends and opportunities

In the age of Big Data, the use of data analytics has become a crucial element for companies in all industries. It allows companies to identify market trends and opportunities, optimise internal processes and make informed decisions for the future of their business.

Data can come from many sources, including sales, social media, surveys and industry data.

Data analysis provides key insights into customers, competitors and market trends. This information is essential to affect strategic decisions, improve products and services and remain competitive.

Businesses can use a variety of tools and software packages to analyse effectively data. Some of the most common include spreadsheets, statistical processing software, data visualisation tools and digital marketing platforms.

Depending on your budget, I recommend that you draw from the list below:

1. **Tableau**: This data visualisation software offers the ability to convert information into interactive graphs and dashboards. It greatly simplifies the understanding and examination of data.

2. **Microsoft Excel**: A spreadsheet program from the Microsoft Office suite, it offers users the ability to generate and review information. Whether for simple analyses, graphs or pivot tables, this tool is perfectly suited to simulating different scenarios.

3. **Google Analytics**: a web analytics tool that provides statistics on traffic, traffic sources and website performance, as well as the ability to measure conversion goals and track traffic trends.

4. **IBM Watson Analytics**: data analysis software that uses artificial intelligence to provide insights from data. It allows you to visualise and explore data, create forecasting models and identify market trends.

5. **R**: This language facilitates the analysis and manipulation of data through statistical programming. It is widely used in research and data analysis, and has a large community of developers who share open-source libraries and tools.

6. **SAS**: data analysis software that provides tools for statistical analysis, predictive modelling and data mining. It is widely used in companies for market research and profitability analysis.

7. **Power BI**: Microsoft's business intelligence tool that creates interactive dashboards to visualise data. Business reporting and data analyses use it to analyse market trends and measure ROI.

To present a successful data analysis strategy, one must first identify the objectives of the analysis. Afterwards, they should determine what data sources are necessary, determine which tools and techniques are best to use, and assign roles to those responsible for collecting and analysing the data.

Certainly, the quality of these data remains a major factor in the veracity of the conclusions.

Definition of CRM (or Customer Relationship Management) :

CRM is a set of strategies, tools and practices that enable companies to better understand and meet the needs of their customers. CRM has become increasingly important over the years, as customers increasingly expect personalised and transparent interactions with companies.

The three main components of this system are customer interaction management, data management, and data analysis:

- Customer **interaction management** is about ensuring that every interaction with the customer is positive and satisfying, using channels such as call centres, social networks and email.

- **Customer data management is the** collection, storage and management of all customer data, such as contact information, purchase history and personal preferences.

- **Customer data analysis is the** use of customer data to understand market trends, preferences and needs to tailor products, services and communications accordingly.

CRM is a continuous process that requires close collaboration between different stakeholders in the company, including marketing, sales, customer service, technical support and IT. Companies frequently use CRM tools and software to automate processes and centralise data, saving time and efficiency.

This component is crucial for businesses, as it helps build customer loyalty, improve customer satisfaction and boost sales. By providing a personalised, quality customer experience, companies can differentiate themselves from their competitors and enhance their reputation.

Depending on the size of your company and the budget for a GRC, I offer you:

➢ For large companies with a larger budget:

1. **Salesforce**: a popular and market-leading platform offering advanced contact management, sales, customer service and marketing capabilities.

2. **HubSpot CRM**: an all-in-one contact management and marketing automation solution, offering a complete suite of tools for sales, customer service and marketing management.

3. **Microsoft Dynamics 365**: a suite of business management solutions, including a complete platform for sales, marketing and customer service management.

4. **SAP CRM**: an enterprise solution that provides marketing, sales and customer service functionality, as well as campaign management and analytics.

5. **Oracle CX Cloud**: a cloud platform offering sales, marketing and customer service solutions, as well as data analysis and reporting capabilities.

➤ For small companies with a smaller budget:
1. **Zoho CRM**: a contact management, sales and customer service platform, offering basic functionality and affordable pricing for small businesses.

2. **Insightly**: a solution offering contact, sales and project management capabilities, as well as integration with marketing and customer support tools.

3. **Agile CRM**: a complete platform, offering marketing, sales and customer service functionality, as well as a project management system and data analysis tools.

4. **Freshworks CRM**: a cloud-based solution, offering contact management, sales and customer service functionality, as well as marketing automation and reporting tools.

5. **Capsule CRM**: a simple contact and sales management solution, offering basic functionality for small businesses, as well as integration with marketing and customer support tools.

Definition of MIS (or Integrated Management System) :

A management information system (MIS) is a software that centralised and integrates all the management activities of a company into a single system. This complete solution enables the company to manage its processes effectively and efficiently, facilitating communication between departments and bolstering decision-making.

MIS typically integrates the following functions: customer relationship management (CRM), supply chain management (SCM), production management (ERP), human resources management (HRM) and accounting/finance. By integrating these different functions, MIS enables the company to work more efficiently and optimise its processes.

The company can customise the GIS to fit their needs and the demands of their industry. Users can access the system either by installing it on an in-house server or by deploying it in the cloud. The benefits of GIS are numerous, including better data management, improved internal communication, reduced costs and increased productivity.

However, implementing a GIS can be complex and requires an investment in time and money. It is therefore important to think carefully about the needs of the business and to work with experts to ensure a successful and efficient implementation.

The choice of a GIS will depend on the five constraints of the company:

1. **The needs and objectives of the company**: The needs of each company and the objectives they wish to fulfil differ. Some MIS are more suitable for a production-based company, while others are more suitable for a service-based company.

2. **The size of the company**: GIS for large companies may be too complex or too expensive for a small company, while GIS for small companies may not offer enough functionality for a larger company.

3. **The nature of the company's business**: some industries have specific management requirements, such as supply chain management or human resource management.

4. **Compatibility with existing systems**: the chosen GIS must be compatible with the other systems in place in the company, to facilitate integration and information exchange.

5. **Company budget**: the cost of a GIS can vary considerably depending on the functionality offered, the size of the company and the complexity of the system. It is important to choose a GIS that fits the company's budget.

Below, you will find the two best MIS for the company, depending on its size:

Name	International company		Local company
FunCoop	SAP S/4HANA Agriculture		Zoho Creator
	Microsoft Dynamics 365 for Agriculture		Odoo
OrAlu	Epicor ERP		QuickBooks Desktop
	SAP Business One		Acumatica
AtlFish	Sage X3		Sage 50cloud
	NetSuite		QuickBooks Online
HighSeaCo	SAP S/4HANA Oil & Gas		Sage 100cloud
	Oracle JD Edwards EnterpriseOne		Zoho Books
DeliFreez	SAP S/4HANA		Dolibarr
	Oracle NetSuite		Odoo
LuxCars	Infor CloudSuite Industrial		Zoho One
	Microsoft Dynamics 366		QuickBooks
PillLab	Epicor ERP		xTuple
	Sage X3		Acumatica
WoodCo	IFS Applications		MRPeasy
	QAD Adaptive ERP		Katana
VIPBank	Salesforce		Odoo
	Microsoft Dynamics 365		Zoho
ColiShip	SAP S/4HANA		Bitrix24
	Oracle NetSuite		SuiteCRM
LearnHub	Microsoft Dynamics 365		Odoo
	Infor		Zoho
WarAid	Salesforce		Bitrix24
	SAP S/4HANA		SuiteCRM

2. Using CRM tools to improve customer relations

CRM tools improve enterprise resource planning (ERP) systems' strategic decision-making abilities. By collecting customer data, these solutions enable them to have a better understanding of their needs and expectations.

Additionally, companies can regularly evaluate their products and services, identify market trends and mutually satisfy all types of business objectives in the short or long term.

To this end, access to relevant analyses via this technology contributes significantly to increasing the overall performance of organisations by optimising the making or even anticipating certain key decisions relating to future business success.

Businesses can leverage their customers' preferences and buying behaviour to tailor their offerings, helping to build loyalty and consumer satisfaction.

Here is how it can help:

1. Gather customers and prospect information in one place so that sales and marketing teams can get a complete picture of their relationship with each customer and better understand their needs and expectations.

2. Facilitate communication with customers and prospects via different channels (e-mail, telephone, social networks, etc.). This allows teams to interact with customers in a personalised and efficient way.

3. Optimally, manage prospects to accurately classify them, and then assign them to sales teams based on their profile and behaviour.

4. Plan sales actions (calls, appointments, follow-ups, etc.) for each customer or prospect to optimise sales follow-up and not miss an opportunity. In this way, you will maintain quality relations with each of your customers.

However, for CRM to be useful, the quality of the entries is crucial. Here is why:

- **The reliability of data**: customer information needs to be accurate and up to date so that sales and marketing teams can use it effectively.

- **Data analysis**: to identify market trends and opportunities, data must be consistent and structured. Teams must ensure they follow the correct data entry fields and formats to enable easy exploitation of data.

- **Communication with customers and regulators**: if the data is incorrect, this can cause miscommunication with customers, which can damage the business relationship. For regulators; the error can have a significant impact on reputation and result in financial penalties or even termination of business.

3. Use process optimisation techniques to improve the efficiency of your business

To achieve process optimisation in the company, follow the steps below:

- The company should recognise the processes necessary for its efficient functioning and pinpoint sections where improvement is essential.

- The process should be analysed to discover which steps are unnecessary or inefficient.

- Formulate an upgrading plan with clear objectives and an assessment scheme to achieve these.

- To implement the necessary changes, apply tools such as project management software and change management techniques.

- Measure progress and make changes based on the results.

4. Use customer loyalty techniques to improve customer retention

By generating emotional bonds with existing customers, we provide the opportunity to enjoy optimal performance and convenience by retaining our customer base rather than seeking to obtain new customers.

This loyalty consists of encouraging the systematic purchase of the products or services offered.

Here are the best solutions for building customer loyalty:

- **Provide high-quality, personalised service**: offer exceptional service and respond quickly and effectively to their questions and concerns. Offer products or services of the highest quality.

- **Reward your customers for their loyalty**: Rewards in the form of points, discounts, gifts or other benefits encourage customers to support your business and consume your products.

- **Ensure excellent after-sales service**: By providing superior after-sales service, you will increase the likelihood that your customers will return to make further purchases.

- **Develop tailor-made communication strategies for each customer**: Provide each customer with a personalised shopping experience by collecting and analysing their shopping behaviour data.

- **Ensure that there is a constant dialogue between stakeholders**: Send newsletters, reminder emails, special promotions or simply messages thanking them for their support, without crossing the line into advertising harassment.

- **Be sensitive and introspective in understanding the needs of your stakeholders**: Enhance your products or services, or simply respond to feedback proactive.

5. Use customer segmentation to target the most profitable customers

Companies divide their customers into distinct groups by analysing their characteristics and buying behaviour. This strategy then allows us to study the specific needs and expectations of each group so that we can design more targeted and relevant offers to reach these customers.

There are several methods of customer segmentation, such as geographical, demographic, behavioural, and psychographic or portfolio weight segmentation. The choice of the method depends on the objectives and characteristics of the company and its customers.

Here are some best practices for using customer segmentation to target the most profitable customers:

- **Interpret information collected from customers**: Collect data on customers such as their buying habits, order history, geographical location and online behaviour. CRM tools are a valuable tool for effective data collection and use.

- **Identify the most profitable customer groups**: Identify high-value customer groups with high revenue-generating potential for the business by analysing their data.

- **Tailor products and services to meet specific customer needs**: Identified customers will benefit from personalised offers of products and services designed to meet their specific needs. For example, offer premium products to wealthier customers or promotions to repeat buyers.

- **Revise marketing communication techniques to ensure better consideration of recipients' needs**: develop personalised marketing communications that address the unique interests and needs of each customer segment. Depending on age, geographic location, interests or buying behaviour, one can customize these messages.

- **Create targeted communication solutions**: offer a personalised customer experience that meets the specific needs of each customer group. For example, offer fast delivery services for the most loyal customers or a discount on their annual fee.

- **Be innovative and creative to improve the quality and effectiveness of communications**: Analyse data to identify buying trends and predict future customer behaviour. By using these tools, companies gain insight into consumer expectations and needs to design an appropriate response.

Many companies have successfully applied customer segmentation to increase their turnover and profitability.

For example, Amazon uses customer segmentation to offer personalised product recommendations based on each customer's previous purchases. Airbnb uses geographic segmentation to provide travel and accommodation offers tailored to the specific interests and needs of travellers.

Companies can use predictive analysis tools to forecast future results based on historical data and complex mathematical models. These tools are available on the market to assist companies with predicting their future outcomes.

Here are some of the best predictive analysis tools:

- IBM SPSS: widely used statistical software that allows researchers to conduct quantitative analysis and research. It helps organise, analyse and interpret information so that the results are valid and explainable. This solution can help you extract valuable research information for your company or institution, such as classified decision tree models, multiple logistic regression, or multidimensional factor analysis. Data can be organised in different formats (pivot tables) that are faster and easier for the public to understand. With the powerful algorithmic engine built into IBM SPSS Statistic, comprehensive reports on the quantitative base help guide your business strategies.

- SAS Predictive Analytics: this machine-learning tool enables companies and researchers to benefit from advanced algorithms, which allow for the analysis of data collected and processed to predict events and uncover trends. This tool gives them more accurate insights, enabling them to make better decisions. By analysing past behaviour, this method helps forecast future behaviour and enables businesses to create better strategies.

- RapidMiner: a data analysis and machine-learning tool that allows users to find hidden patterns in their data. This solution automates their analytical process to make decisions more informed in marketing, sales, and even in continuous product improvement. Users can use this tool to do predictive analysis, uncover the implications of raw data, create machine learning-based models and generate graphical representations based on user input.

- Microsoft Azure Machine Learning: a data science platform that provides a powerful set of tools for analysing and developing artificial intelligence-based applications. It allows users to create models, such as deep neural networks, from unstructured or structured data to predict future trends and provide actionable insights.

- Alteryx: a business intelligence and analytics platform, it enables companies to collect, merge, cleanse and analyse their data using a powerful and intuitive engine. Data manipulation, advanced statistics, workflows, and visualisation and sharing are all practical features that make it easier to leverage information for informed decisions. The platform can improve the quality of the decision-making process through its analytical tool, enabling users to communicate more effectively within their organisation. Alteryx provides an extraordinary platform that allows employees with different levels of knowledge and skills to interpret simultaneously the extracted data to make better decisions through collaboration on their perspectives.

Offering a huge variety of features and adaptable to various industries and business needs, these tools offer companies the opportunity to choose the most appropriate one considering cost, functionality and ease of use.

6. **Use testing and iteration methods to improve your business results**

To be successful, companies must constantly improve their performance. To achieve this goal, they should implement testing and iteration methods to evaluate the effectiveness of strategies and ideas, changing what does not work based on the results. This improves their processes and exploits their full potential.

Here are some of the best practices for using testing and iteration methods in your business:

- **Establish defined and measurable objectives.** Before conducting a test, outline the objectives clearly to ensure that desired results can be achieved. Testing can be directed with help, allowing the accuracy of its effectiveness to be assessed.

- **Gather information**: to evaluate the effectiveness of a test, collect accurate and reliable data. Data can come from online monitoring tools, customer questionnaires, or field tests.

- **Explore the implications of each result**: after collecting the data, examine it in depth to draw useful conclusions. Compare the results to your original goals to assess the effectiveness of the test.

- **Suggest improvements**: by analysing the results, you can introduce changes to your strategy or product to improve continuously its performance.

- **Repeat the cycle**: after making changes, evaluate the effectiveness of the changes by re-running the testing and iteration process.

- **Use quantitative analysis methods to capture relevant information**: To facilitate data collection and analysis, use data analysis tools such as Google Analytics, KISSmetrics or Mixpanel.

- **Encourage collaboration between different team members**: for the testing and iteration process to be effective, involve all team members, including marketers, developers and designers.

This practice has yielded successful examples. Additionally, these examples demonstrate the effectiveness of this approach:

1. **Booking.com**: The hotel-booking site Booking.com uses A/B testing to improve the performance of their site. They regularly test different elements of their site, such as button colours, headlines and images, to determine which variation works best with users. These tests have helped Booking.com to improve significantly their conversion rates.

2. **Spotify**: The music streaming service Spotify also uses testing and iteration methods to improve their user experience. They conducted A/B testing to determine which changes in their user interface have a positive impact on user engagement. For example, they have tested

different playlist layouts to determine which works best for users. These tests have allowed Spotify to optimise their user interface and improve their retention rate.

3. **Zalando**: The online shopping platform Zalando uses performance testing to improve the performance of their website. The site speed analysis tools allow them to identify which pages take the longest to load. They then work to optimise these pages to improve the speed of their site and provide a better user experience. Because of these tests, Zalando has been able to reduce its site load time and improve customer satisfaction.

5   SUSTAINABILITY AND ENVIRONMENTAL RESPONSIBILITY

1.   Reducing the carbon footprint

Reducing the carbon footprint has become a major concern for companies in all sectors. As well as being a legal requirement in many countries, reducing your company's environmental impact can also provide competitive advantages, improve brand image and contribute to the long-term sustainability of the business.

The use of renewable energy sources, such as solar or wind power, to power their operations is still a used solution. Digital technology and automation generally result in lower energy requirements.

The company can also improve the energy efficiency of their machinery and production process, using state-of-the-art technology to minimise waste. By also reducing employee travel, through teleworking, the premises need less water, electricity and heating.

2.   Use renewable energy sources to reduce your company's energy costs and environmental impact.

The use of renewable energy has become a major concern for many companies concerned about their environmental impact and the control of their energy costs.

Renewable energies such as solar, wind, hydro and geothermal energy can help address this dual problem.

Here are some tips for an effective strategy:

- **Analyse energy needs**: before investing in renewable energy solutions, it is essential to analyse your company's energy needs. Determining the exact amount of energy needed by the company, how long it needs to be used, and where a considerable benefit can be achieved are crucial.

- **Investing in energy-efficient equipment**: reducing energy costs also means using energy-efficient equipment. Companies can opt for energy-efficient equipment such as LED light bulbs, air conditioners or energy-efficient heaters.

- **Installing solar panels or wind turbines**: Renewable energies such as solar or wind power are interesting alternatives to reduce the company's energy costs while limiting the environmental impact. Companies can install solar panels on the roofs of buildings or on land close to their own premises, while areas with high wind exposure are ideal for installing wind turbines.

- **Using geothermal energy sources or biomass**: Geothermal heat pumps offer companies an interesting solution to heat and cool their buildings, ecologically and with savings. Additionally, biomass can produce thermal or electrical energy as a source.

- **Supporting renewable energy projects**: Companies can also support renewable energy projects by investing in renewable energy generation projects or by purchasing renewable energy from green electricity suppliers.

3. **Using energy efficiency to reduce your company's operating costs**

Energy efficiency not only lowers operating costs, but also reduces the environmental impact of business operations.

To achieve this objective, it is wise to perform an energy audit to detect weak points and identify appropriate solutions. The company can conduct this analysis itself or hire a specialist company for the task.

Second, one can implement energy efficiency measures. The most common solutions include:

- **Thermal insulation**: With good insulation, you can keep warm in winter and avoid excessive temperatures in summer.

- **The use of energy-efficient heating, ventilation and air-conditioning (HVAC) systems**: The careful selection of energy-efficient HVAC equipment is essential to reduce the overall consumption of the buildings.

- **The use of LED lighting**: LED bulbs offer advantages such as energy savings and a longer life span compared to traditional bulbs.

- **Implementing an energy management system**: using an energy management system, one can identify and address any misuses of resources by monitoring and controlling energy consumption.

- **Employee training**: educating employees on the importance of energy efficiency can reduce behavioural energy waste.

4. **Use environmental assessments to identify areas of your business that need improvement in terms of environmental impact**

Companies have a considerable role to play in protecting the environment. To reduce their environmental impact, they can use environmental assessments to identify areas for improvement. This approach allows companies to identify their company's environmental problems, develop strategies to address them, and continue to make progress over time.

Environmental assessment is a process by which a company examines the environmental impact of its activities. It identifies the areas that have the greatest impact on the environment and designs strategies to reduce that impact.

Identifying the company's environmental impacts, analysing the risks and defining corrective measures are all parts of the assessment process. Once this is done, the implementation follows.

Companies can use effective tools and methods such as life cycle assessments, environmental audits and sustainability assessments to do this.

The best practices for companies to apply are:

- **Establish a strong environmental commitment**: commit to reducing the environmental impact by adopting sustainable business practices and implementing measures for improvement.

- **Develop an environmental action plan**: develop a detailed environmental action plan that includes specific objectives and measures.

- **Measure results**: carry out regular checks on environmental performance to verify progress and ensure that the measures applied are effective.

- **Involve employees**: provide employees with the necessary training and relevant tools to enable them to participate actively in efforts to reduce environmental impact.

- **Collaborate with stakeholders**: develop strategies jointly with customers, suppliers and local communities to boost their environmental effectiveness.

5. Establish a corporate culture of sustainability to encourage employees to adopt environmentally friendly practices

Today, more and more companies are committing to adopting environmentally friendly practices in response to environmental challenges. To achieve this transition, companies must develop a corporate culture that focuses on sustainability.

Businesses should understand that sustainability is not an additional expense, but rather an opportunity for innovation and opportunity. Indeed, the participatory adoption of sustainable ways of doing business allows them to reduce costs, boost productivity and enhance credibility.

To develop a corporate culture focused on sustainability, follow these guidelines:

- **Educate employees on environmental issues**: employees must understand how their contribution can have a positive impact on the environment and why sustainability is so important. Training, workshops or seminars can be an excellent way to raise awareness of environmental issues.

- **Create clear environmental objectives**: to support sustainable development, set clear environmental objectives. These objectives should be achievable and measurable, whether it is a reduction in greenhouse gases, less waste or a good optimisation of energy use.

- **Integrate sustainability into operational processes**: operational decisions should consider their environmental effects, including raw material sourcing and product delivery.

- **Encourage environmental innovation**: use more technologies that are efficient, incorporate recyclable materials and optimise production processes to enhance your energy balance.

- **Create a reward system**: unifying company goals with sustainable practices, invite all employees to join the effort to respect the environment. To motivate and support your employees in this area, offer various incentives for good offices. This can be through financial incentives for those who implement sustainable practices or paid time off for personal environmental projects.

- **Partner with environmental organisations**: partnerships can help you make a bigger difference in the environment through restoration projects, awareness-raising campaigns and volunteer programmes.

6. **Use communication to raise awareness of your company's sustainable practices among customers and partners**

Raising awareness can help improve your brand image and strengthen your commitment to the environment. Here, we explore the unique ways in which companies can use communication to promote their sustainable practices.

- **Highlight your commitment to the environment in your communication**: include information about your sustainable practices in your internal and external communications. This can be in your newsletter, on your website, in your advertising, etc.

- **Share testimonials and inspirational stories**: spread these stories across all your communication channels to inspire your customers and partners.

- **Promote awareness-raising events**: organise open days to present your company, organise events to inform customers about your sustainable products and offer conferences to highlight your commitment to the environment.

- **Offer rewards**: Reward your customers for practising environmentally responsible behaviour or recommending your environmentally friendly products to motivate them to continue these initiatives.

- **Collaborate with partners**: make a commitment to the environment, but also make it known that this priority is an important asset for your company. This will increase and strengthen your brand image.

6   ANALYSIS OF STRENGTHS AND WEAKNESSES

1. Identify the strengths and weaknesses of your business

Every company has its strengths and weaknesses. This is an unavoidable reality. Nevertheless, recognising and understanding these strengths and weaknesses can help reinforce the positive aspects and work on the negative aspects to improve the whole business.

Identifying the strengths and weaknesses of your business requires a thorough and objective analysis of all aspects of the company. Strengths can be in the form of excellent product or service quality, a recognised brand reputation, satisfied customers, positive financial returns, high levels of competence among staff or an inspiring climate within the organisation itself.

Be aware of the weaknesses that can affect your organisation, such as quantitative problems in internal communication with business partners, high production costs, possible profitability losses or managerial failures. These could compromise your day-to-day operations.

Carefully analysing all aspects, even the smallest ones, is essential to get a complete picture of the company (the devil is in the details). During this study, it is important to stay honest with ourselves in order for the process to be objective. Our strengths can hide our weaknesses, and our weaknesses can conceal our strengths.

OO + NT = EOO

Old Organization + New Technology = Expensive Old Organization

44

I recommend that you take this route to achieve the desired goal:

- **Conduct a SWOT analysis** (strengths, weaknesses, opportunities, threats): With this method, you determine the internal and external elements that may affect your business.

- **Carry out market research**: This analysis will provide a better understanding of the market in which you operate, the needs of your customers and the strategies implemented by your competitors.

- **Conduct a financial analysis**: Determine the financial health and profitability of your company.

- **Survey your employees**: Employees can offer a distinct view of your business and allow you to identify problems or opportunities that might otherwise go unnoticed.

- **Seek advice from external consultants**: External experts provide an unbiased view of your company's strengths and weaknesses and can put in place strategies to mitigate them. The outside perspective can offer a new and constructive view of how your organisation operates.

2. Using customer feedback to improve your business

Frankly, customer feedback! What a wonderful way to improve your business. They are like jewels in a coal mine, stars in a dark sky, and lifelines for your distressed business. You cannot ignore them because they can still be the starting point for considerable improvement.

Nevertheless, how can you use them effectively? Here are some tips to help you make the most of customer feedback.

First, it is essential to listen carefully to what customers have to say. Do not interrupt them, do not minimise their experience, and do not dismiss them. Listen carefully because there may be something valuable to discover.

Second, do not take customer feedback lightly. Take it seriously and act on it. If a customer complains about a problem, find a solution to fix it. If a customer suggests an improvement, really consider it and implement it if possible.

Third, use customer feedback as an opportunity to connect with them. Show them that you care about their experience and that you are willing to try to improve things. This can greatly improve customer loyalty and trust in your business.

Overall, do not forget to praise customers for their feedback. Whether online or in person, show them that you value their time and thoughts. This can help strengthen customer relationships and encourage more feedback in the future.

- **Implement a feedback strategy**: systematically and conduct regularly online surveys, satisfaction polls, obtain feedback from social networks or other online review sites, etc.

- **Analyse customer feedback**: identify trends, recurring problems, strengths and weaknesses in your business using data analysis tools to improve your processes.

- **Actto solve identified problems**: for example, if customers complain that your service is slow, act to improve the speed of the service.

- **Involve your employees**: ask your employees to participate actively by offering ideas and suggestions for improving your company's products and services.

- **Communicate with customers**: let your customers know that you have considered their feedback and are committed to improving your company. This strongly suggests that you care about their views and demonstrates your commitment to delivering exceptional customer service.

- **Track results**: Measure the results of your efforts by tracking key performance indicators (KPIs) such as customer satisfaction rate, customer retention rate, conversion rate, etc. This will allow you to measure the impact of your strategy and take steps to continue to improve based on customer feedback. This will allow you to measure the impact of your strategy and take steps to continue improving based on customer feedback.

3. Using competitive analysis to identify opportunities

Competitive analysis is a systematic approach that looks in depth at the strengths and weaknesses of your competitors in the industry. This analysis helps to identify opportunities and threats that your company may face. Devise more strategies, successful by gaining a more in-depth understanding of your competitive environment to increase your market share and profitability.

For example, in the smartphone industry, Apple and Samsung are direct competitors. By studying their marketing strategies, product ranges, pricing and distribution channels, a company looking to enter this market can identify opportunities to differentiate itself and offer benefits to consumers.

Here are some tips for conducting an effective competitive analysis:

- **Identify your direct competitors**: To assess your market position, it is essential to know and analyse your competitors. Make a list of competing companies and examine their size, market share, marketing strategies, product or service offerings, competitive advantages, etc.

- **Analyse their marketing strategy**: Look at how your competitors communicate with their target audience, the distribution channels they use, the prices they charge, etc. This will allow you to determine the strengths and weaknesses of their marketing strategy and compare it with yours. This will allow you to determine the strengths and weaknesses of their marketing strategy and compare it with yours.

- **Analyse their product or service offering**: Examine competitors' product and service offerings, including their quality, innovation and pricing. This will give you a look at their strengths and weaknesses, so you can determine how you can make a greater difference on your side.

- **Analyse their competitive advantage**: Assess the strength of your competitors and determine why customers choose to do business with them. Use this information to create opportunities that will create a differentiated, profitable offering.

- **Assessing market trends**: Conduct competitive intelligence to keep abreast of the latest market trends and innovations from your competitors. This will allow you to anticipate future market developments and identify opportunities.

Here are some of the best competitive analysis tools available in the market:

1. SEMrush: This SEO and online marketing tool provides detailed data on competitors, making it easy to compare them and identify opportunities. SEMRush has a powerful SEO auditing tool that provides information on the quality of a site's organic SEO, including associated technical errors and missing keywords compared to its competitors, among others. It also offers ranking reports from multiple sources so that SEO specialists can get a rich overview with nearly 200 different levels for further analysis. Finally, with SEMRush Organic Research On Page, it is possible to not only observe but also compare the content produced by competitors dedicated to target audiences or to be optimised over time to impress Google rankers.

2. Rival IQ: is a competitive analysis tool that provides companies with a visual presentation of social media data and competitive insights. It allows users to monitor social media activity, performance and engagement for their own brand and those of their competitors. Advanced analytics can help analyse how to stand out on social platforms to create more effective and targeted campaigns. Additionally, Rival IQ also offers customisable content to understand comparative performance positioning, which helps identify strategic opportunities specific to each sector or business.

3. Brandwatch: is a social intelligence platform based on the use of AI technology to collect accurate data from social media, the web, and other sources. This allows companies to monitor their key competitors in real time so that they can uncover new and relevant future trends. Brandwatch technology allows companies to more clearly understand how customers interact with their brands using advanced natural language that captures all product or service related content across all available digital platforms. Detailed statistical analysis can provide a comprehensive view of the competition, and identifying potential business opportunities that

lie behind the words or phrases used by the target market will require combining it with linguistic analysis.

4. Owler: is a competitive analysis tool that helps companies identify trends and opportunities in their market by monitoring nearly 15 million global companies and brands. It allows companies to observe the competitive strategy of others, giving them a head start in strategically positioning themselves in their respective markets. Owler also provides detailed industry information, market size, and relevant financial and business information. Additionally, it offers clear insights based on artificial intelligence to help companies plan their future business activities correctly.

5. SpyFu: allows its users to monitor competitors' marketing strategies and SEO, retrieving monthly data that helps to understand what your competitors are doing to attract traffic. This can be useful for identifying potential business opportunities from a linguistic and communication perspective. It also allows businesses to perform comparative analyses based on current and past trends, as well as full monitoring of powerful Google Keyword details via the AdWords Integration API. You can use this information to build your online presence effectively and tailor your content to suit the best practise, accurately target a particular market or adjust your brand to meet shifting consumer needs.

6. Moz Pro: is an integrated data management and analytics platform that includes advanced tools to help businesses better understand their competitors and discover more opportunities. Using MozPro, brands can collect, analyse and generate automated reports based on SEO activity, online advertising techniques, organic search via a paid/free report, referral traffic (backlinks) and many other relevant statistics about their competitors. You can predict how your business compares with your competitors so that your business can reach its full potential.

4. Use market testing to validate your product or service

By taking advantage of market testing, companies can reduce their investment risk and ensure that their products or services meet customer needs and expectations. Market testing can provide many benefits to organisations. It can help them to identify and assess opportunities, as well as improve their processes and products.

What is a market test?

Before launching a product or service on the market, it is important to perform a market test. Consumers will enthusiastically receive this study and provide valuable feedback about it. Potential customers give their opinion on a product or service in a small sample. Ask them to share their opinions and recommendations for improvement. The study identifies potential market targets, measures the appeal of the product or service, and determines what changes are necessary.

Why conduct a market test?

Market testing is useful for several reasons:

- **Validate the product or service**: before introducing a product or service to the market, companies should conduct market testing to gauge its potential levels of attractiveness and relevance.

- **Identify market targets**: market research helps us identify the needs and expectations of potential customers, while determining which market segments are most relevant to our product or service.

- **Reduce launch risks**: by assessing the response of potential customers, market testing can minimise the financial and image risks associated with a product or service.

How to conduct a market test?

Here are some key steps for conducting an effective market test:

1. **Define the objective of the market test**: the clear objective of the market test is to analyse the reaction of potential customers to a new product or service.

2. **Identify selection criteria**: identify your target audience by choosing a suitable sample, considering factors such as gender, age, place of residence, income, portfolio and occupation.

3. **Design the survey**: create a questionnaire to collect feedback from potential customers, including open and closed questions to obtain qualitative and quantitative feedback.

4. **Collect the data**: collect feedback from the sample of potential customers.

5. **Analyse the data**: determine the strengths and weaknesses of the product or service, the most appropriate market segments and the necessary modifications.

The best solutions for market testing

There are several solutions for market testing, here are some of the best:

- SurveyMonkey: is an excellent tool for validating a product or service with the target audience. It can be an online survey, with short, specific questions, that allows professionals to ask the right questions and gather the feedback needed to validate a product or service. The data obtained through SurveyMonkey allows companies to adjust their offerings based on the feedback collected so that they are more appropriate for the target market. You can also use it to measure the psychographic profile of respondents, which can be very useful when it comes to getting to know your audience better before a specific marketing campaign.

- Google Analytics: is a free and handy tool that provides you with detailed information about your users' behaviour. It can measure the engagement, performance and traffic of the website or application you are in analysis. This allows businesses to gain a better understanding of consumers' buying habits, which in turn will improve communication with them, as well as the implementation of more effective marketing strategies. Google Analytics is not just about providing quantitative feedback; it is also about identifying the channels that deliver the highest return on investment (ROI), double-clicking to drill down into each activity and getting immediate statistical analysis. This means that all this information is easily accessible directly from your web browser! With Google Analytics, your product or service will be testable and adaptable to the current market requirements. Your business will then have even more opportunities to grow!

- UserTesting: is a practical and useful tool for validating products or services. It offers quality tests, which can be carried out by demographically diverse users (age, gender and socio-economic level). Companies can obtain both quantitative and qualitative data about the advantages and shortcomings of a specific product or service from UserTesting. This information can be beneficial before implementation, giving them invaluable insights to aid informed decision-making. The data collected allows companies to improve their marketing strategy while optimising the customer experience at every stage of the process. Finally, this tool facilitates the rapid identification of potential product problems. With user testing, organisations can ensure that their products meet market expectations before they go to the market.

- Testapic: is an online trend analysis tool that allows companies and product designers to generate quickly insights about their customers. It offers the ability to collect, organise and analyse data from both the web and user testing to get a complete view of the market. Testapic also provides detailed information about consumer practices, expectations and behaviour specific to a given sector or region so that companies can shape their marketing strategy accordingly. Testing with Testapic can help validate whether your product meets the current market needs while providing a quick and cost-effective way to collect this information.

- Amazon Mechanical Turk: developers and entrepreneurs can take advantage of this great opportunity to obtain fast, objective data for their products or services. Indeed, Amazon Mechanical Turk is a platform that provides easy access to a wide range of qualified people from worldwide. Users can then receive objective feedback on the products or services they are offering so that they can check the demand and adjust their business strategy accordingly. Additionally, the use of Amazon mechanical Turk will allow companies and startups to reduce the costs associated with acquiring, processing and analysing the new data generated by this innovative technique.

- A/B testing: is one of the most effective and affordable ways to test the relevance of your product or service to your prospects. This form of testing involves simultaneously testing different versions of a web page (version A and B) or marketing campaign to allow companies to gain insight into their target audience. Depending on the results, they can determine which version is more attractive and effective and improve their web marketing strategy. As a result, it is possible not only to develop a better customer experience, but also to significantly increase ROI (Return On Investment).

5. Using cost analysis to identify areas for cost reduction

Follow a formal decision-making process to ensure cost efficiency. This will help to maximize the benefits. It is important to identify precisely all the costs associated with the production and launch of the product or service. These include materials for manufacturing, as well as the personnel required, and the budget for promotion and marketing to get it to market. Packaging and transport should be included in the final account.

Estimate all the cumulative costs, then set a reasonable price ceiling to maximise the return on investment. By regularly monitoring, we can ensure that we reach our planned targets according to the original plan.

With this list of costs, it is crucial to analyse their effects on the profitability of the business. Examine unit costs, comparing expenses and sales profits in detail. Identify which costs can be reduced without impairing the product/service quality and performance. Assess the effects that reducing these costs would have on your business.

To help companies perform effective cost analysis, many tools and software are available on the market:

- **QuickBooks**: is easy-to-use online software that can help businesses manage their finances and improve the efficiency of their cost management. It includes various tools for tracking expenses, reporting and forecasting budgets, so you can see exactly where every dollar is going and how it can be reduced. When coupled with in-depth analysis of your financial data, QuickBooks provides companies with excellent visibility into their spending and the ability to find quickly reasonable ways to meet their budgetary goals.

- **Zoho Books**: another online accounting software that can be used to improve cost decision-making. It offers powerful tools to help analyse and manage finances, create easily understandable reports, monitor cash flow and generate quick budget estimates. With ZohoBooks, you can also easily track all your expenses over a period to identify quickly where you can cut costs. All of this means that ZohoBooks is perfectly suited to those who want to optimise their budget through effective cost-benefit analysis.

- **Excel**: although not specifically designed for cost analysis, there are many advantages to using Excel for cost analysis. First, Excel can easily handle complex data and provide in-depth and detailed analysis in a relatively short time. With its built-in features such as the pivot table, it offers the ability to group, sort and consolidate large amounts of data to obtain meaningful results. Additionally, Excel also has built-in charts that allow users to visualise their results quickly and accurately. This software tool is powerful because it offers various customisable "tuning" options that greatly facilitate quick comparative analysis between several possible financial or cost reduction scenarios.

- **SAP Business One**: is an integrated management system that enables companies to better analyse costs and reduce expenses. The software offers a full range of cost management capabilities, including advanced analysis tools such as resource allocation and customisable dashboards. With SAP Business One, companies can consolidate and analyse their data from different sources to quickly identify what can be done to improve efficiency. Using the software allows users to increase their visibility in their operational and financial activities, providing a 360-degree view of all aspects of cost management. In this way, SAP Business One helps companies optimise productivity through better cost analysis that can contribute to the ongoing budget reduction.

This analysis usually improves the overall profitability of the company and can help to gain a better position in the market.

6. Using competitive advantages to differentiate your business from the competition

To stand out from the crowd, companies should have strong competitive advantages. To achieve this, they must understand their targets and tailor their products to their needs and desires. Advanced technologies, outsourcing activities and better management are always to reduce costs.

Specific training can boost the quality of the raw materials, thereby improving the company's performance. Additionally, to provide an unforgettable customer experience, you can offer additional support or facilitate feedback and exchange through a mobile application.

Connect with consumers by telling your story to distinguish yourself. Showcase your brand image to create an impact.

7   GROWTH AND ADAPTATION STRATEGIES

1. Use differentiation strategies to distinguish yourself from the competition

Differentiation strategies allow companies to distinguish themselves by offering unique products or services or by designing a distinct brand image. Companies can employ numerous strategies to differentiate themselves. Such strategies can help them stand out from their competitors.

- - Invest in high-quality materials, advanced manufacturing processes and technical expertise to deliver the best possible quality compared to your competitors.

- - By spearheading design, the appearance of their products or services will achieve a unique and attractive look that attracts customers' attention. They can also use packaging to reinforce their brand image and market positioning.

- - With technology, technological innovation can deliver superior products or services. This involves investing in research and development to create unique products or services or to improve existing products or services to make them more efficient.

European companies are known for their use of effective differentiation strategies. In particular, the German car brand Mercedes differentiates itself through the quality of its vehicles and technological innovation. It offers top-of-the-range models with advanced features, such as autonomous driving and connectivity.

The French luxury brand Louis-Vuitton stands out for its unique design and high-end image. It uses high-quality materials and artisanal techniques to develop exclusive and elegant products.

The British cosmetics brand Lush differentiates itself by using natural and sustainable ingredients for its products. It uses recyclable packaging and minimises the use of plastics to reduce the environmental impact.

IKEA differentiates itself through its affordable quality products and functional design. It uses sustainable materials for its furniture and home accessories, while offering modern and practical designs.

2. Use market penetration strategies to reach a wider audience

The market penetration is about convincing new customers or encouraging existing customers to buy more by offering innovative products or services, improving quality or adjusting prices. By adopting effective market penetration strategies, companies can gain awareness, loyalty and market share, contributing to their long-term growth and success.

Thus, Netflix has used market penetration strategies to establish itself as a global leader in video streaming. The company began by delivering mail-order DVD rental service and then moved into online streaming, offering an ever-expanding catalogue of films and TV series. By continually adjusting its offerings and investing heavily in the production of original content, Netflix has been able to reach a wider audience and build subscriber loyalty.

Here are some tips for implementing an effective market penetration strategy:

- **- Lowering prices**: one of the most common ways to implement a market penetration strategy is to lower prices. This can convince new price-sensitive customers and encourage existing customers to buy more. However, this strategy can reduce the company's profit margins, so it is important to make calculations before deciding.

- **- Increase publicity**: another way to attract the attention of a wide audience is to increase publicity. This can include online, television or social media advertising. The aim is to raise the awareness of your business and convince potential customers to buy your products or services.

- **- Explore new distribution channels**: it may be beneficial to explore new distribution channels to reach a wider audience. For example, if your business currently sells only online, you may want to consider marketing your products in physical shops to reach customers who prefer to shop in person.

- **- Giving benefits to existing customers**: it is essential not to neglect existing customers when implementing a market penetration strategy. Offering exclusive discounts or benefits to existing customers can encourage them to buy more products or services and can build long-term loyalty.

3. Use diversification strategies to develop new products or services

By broadening their offering, companies can reduce the risks associated with dependence on a single market, while benefiting from new revenue and growth opportunities. Diversifying can be extremely beneficial when existing markets are declining or saturated, and we want to make the most of our knowledge to seize new opportunities.

Amazon began as an online bookseller, but quickly expanded to offer a wide range of products and services: electronics, clothing, video streaming and web services. Amazon has diversified its business, boosting its power and creating new sources of income to withstand market fluctuations more effectively.

The three best diversification strategies are

1. **Related diversification**: Expand the company's activities into areas related to its core business. For example, a company that manufactures cars may diversify into the manufacture of motorbikes or bicycles.

2. **Horizontal diversification**: Exploit opportunities outside the company's core business to expand its capabilities and contribute to its mission. For example, a company that manufactures pet food may diversify into the manufacture of pet toys.

3. **Conglomerate diversification**: Explore opportunities to expand the company's activities into areas outside its core business. For example, a company that makes shoes may diversify into film production.

Note that diversification can be risky and requires careful planning to succeed. Companies should carefully evaluate diversification opportunities and ensure that they have the resources to succeed in the new market or products.

Company	Ideas for diversification		
	1	2	3
FunCoop	Fruit juice production	Poultry farming	Olive oil production
OrAlu	Solar panel production	Metal recycling	Production of batteries for electric vehicles
AtlFish	Production of prepared fish dishes	Production of pet food	Shrimp farming
HighSeaCo	Biofuel production	Offshore wind	Production of frozen seafood products
DeliFreez	Production of snacks	Beverage production	Production of desserts
LuxCars	Motorbike production	Bicycle design	Development of electric cars
PillLab	Vaccine manufacturing	Antibiotic production	Drug development for rare diseases
WoodCo	Production of kit furniture	Construction of prefabricated houses	Manufacture of energy-efficient windows and doors
VIPBank	Car insurance	Real estate brokerage service	Home insurance
ColiShip	Storage	Fleet management	Transport of dangerous goods
LearnHub	Online certification	In-company training courses	Mentoring platform
WarAid	Provisions of social services to businesses	Sustainable development consultancy	Corporate Volunteering Programme

4. Using consolidation strategies to improve the efficiency of your business

This strategy reorganises the structure to reduce costs and increase operational efficiency. Identify businesses or assets that will strengthen the company's market position and acquire them. Then, evaluate how these acquisitions would benefit the organisation in terms of their overall objectives.

Identify potential targets, and then create an effective acquisition strategy. This may include negotiating contracts, creating alliances or partnerships, or even acquiring competing companies. The company should identify cost-efficient ways to acquire assets and devise strategies to integrate them successfully into its portfolio.

The effective integration of acquired assets is essential to ensure that consolidation has a positive impact on business efficiency. Ensure that fully defined protocols are in place for integrating assets, including the installation of new systems, staff training and the establishment of operational procedures.

On balance, observe and analyse the results of consolidation to assess its impact on business efficiency. This may include measuring market share, reducing costs and analysing financial performance. Be flexible and ready to adjust the consolidation if the results do not meet expectations.

Here are four examples of successful business consolidation:

- The French energy giant Total acquired the battery manufacturer Saft in 2016 for €950 million. The acquisition allowed Total to diversify into the fast-growing battery business while strengthening its position in the renewable energy market.

- In 2018, the Dutch building materials' company Koninklijke BAM acquired the German tunnelling company Wayss & Freytag. This acquisition strengthened BAM's position in the German market and allowed the company to diversify into a new business area.

- In 2015, the Spanish renewable energy group Acciona acquired the German wind turbine company Nordex for €785 million. This acquisition allowed Acciona to strengthen its position in the wind energy market in Europe and to diversify into new markets in Asia and South America.

- In 2019, the German Siemens Group merged its rail division with the French company Alstom to form a new company, Siemens Alstom. The merger created one of the world's largest rail equipment manufacturers, offering a full range of products and services for rail systems.

5. Using cooperation strategies to build beneficial partnerships

Cooperative strategies enable organisations to draw on the skills, resources and knowledge of their partners, creating synergies and mutual benefits. By establishing beneficial partnerships, companies can access new markets, improve their products and service offering and increase their competitiveness.

Cooperation strategies such as joint ventures, strategic alliances, subcontracting partnerships and mergers exist in several forms. Companies can choose the cooperation strategy that best suits their situation and objectives.

- A joint venture is a form of cooperation in which two companies create a separate legal entity to operate a joint project or activity. The companies share the costs, risks and benefits of the joint venture.

- A strategic alliance is a form of cooperation in which two companies join forces to achieve a common goal. The companies retain their legal independence, but work together to develop and market a product or service.

- Subcontracting is a form of cooperation in which one company subcontracts part of its activity to another company. This allows the company to focus on its core competencies and reduce production costs.

- A merger is a form of cooperation in which two companies merge to create one company. This strategy can enable companies to achieve economies of scale, expand their geographical reach and share resources.

The benefits of cooperative strategies can be numerous. Companies can reduce costs by sharing research and development expenses, marketing and production costs. They can also benefit from an increased reach through distribution or marketing partnerships.

However, there are risks to this strategy. Be mindful of cultural compatibility and the management of potential conflicts. Companies should also ensure that the benefits of cooperation outweigh the costs and risks associated with the strategy.

Business-to-business cooperation is a win-win strategy for companies seeking to establish beneficial partnerships.

Here are a few examples of this practice successfully carried out by world-renowned companies.

In the United States, the joint venture between Nestlé and General Mills created Cereal Partners Worldwide. This joint venture allowed the two companies to combine their resources to develop and market breakfast products worldwide.

In Europe, two notable examples of successful strategic alliances are Airbus and Bombardier, which have formed an alliance to produce the CSeries aircraft, and Renault-Nissan-Mitsubishi, which have formed an alliance to share technologies and costs for developing new car models.

In Asia, the outsourcing partnership between Apple and Foxconn has allowed Apple to outsource the production of its iPhones to Foxconn, which can produce massive volumes at low cost.

Finally, two examples of successful mergers include the merger between Dow Chemical and DuPont, which created a combined company with activities in the agricultural, industrial and life sciences sectors, and the merger between Essilor and Luxottica, which created a world leader in the optical industry.

These examples illustrate the importance of cooperation and consolidation for companies seeking to increase efficiency and benefit from mutually beneficial partnerships.

For our basic examples, some ideas:

Company	Joint venture	Strategic alliance	Subcontracting partnership	Merger
FunCoop	Creation of a joint venture with a dairy cooperative to produce premium cheese	Signing of a partnership with a food processing company to expand the product range	Collaboration with a transport company for distributing local products	Merger with a food distribution company to expand the geographic reach
OrAlu	Joint venture with a mining company for the joint operation of a bauxite mine	Signing of a partnership with a recycling company for the recovery of aluminium waste	Collaboration with a logistics company for the transport of raw materials	Merger with an aluminium production company to strengthen the value chain
AtlFish	Joint venture with an aquaculture company for freshwater fish farming	Signing of a partnership with a food processing company for the diversification of seafood products	Collaboration with a logistics company for the export of fresh products	Merger with a food distribution company to strengthen seafood distribution
HighSeaCo	Joint venture with a shipping company for deep-sea fishing	Signing of a partnership with a food preservation company to expand the product range	Collaboration with a logistics company for the transport of fresh products	Merger with a food distribution company to strengthen seafood distribution
DeliFreez	Partner with a transport company to improve the distribution of their frozen products	Partner with a packaging material supplier to reduce costs	Working with a cleaning company to improve hygiene and safety	Merge with a ready meal company to expand their products offering
LuxCars	Working with a battery company to develop more efficient electric cars	Partner with a car rental company to offer long-term rental services	Work with a recycling company to minimise the environmental impact	Merge with a high-end car company to expand their target market

Company	Joint venture	Strategic alliance	Subcontracting partnership	Merger
PillLab	Partnering with a research company to develop new, more effective drugs	Partner with a materials' supplier to reduce production costs	Work with a distribution company to improve the delivery of their products	Merge with a medical device company to expand their product portfolio
WoodCo	Working with a wood treatment company to improve the quality of their products	Partner with a design company to create more innovative furniture	Working with a logistics company to improve the efficiency of their supply chain	Merge with a building materials' company to diversify their products offering
VIPBank	VIPBank and ColiShip have formed a joint venture to offer online money transfer services worldwide.	VIPBank and WarAid have formed an alliance to offer exclusive banking services to war veterans.	VIPBank has entered into an outsourcing partnership with LearnHub to outsource the continuing education of its employees.	VIPBank recently announced a merger with a small local bank, which will allow it to expand its geographical reach and offer more diversified financial services.
ColiShip	ColiShip and FunCoop have formed a joint venture to manage the logistics of raw material supply for companies in the primary sector of the Eric List.	ColiShip and VIPBank have formed a strategic alliance to offer online banking services to ColiShip customers.	ColiShip has established a subcontracting partnership with WarAid to transport medical supplies to war zones.	ColiShip recently merged with an Asian logistics company to expand its presence in Asia and to increase its transport capacity.
LearnHub	LearnHub and WoodCo have formed a joint venture to provide e-learning services for WoodCo employees.	LearnHub and VIPBank have formed a strategic alliance to offer exclusive banking services to LearnHub employees.	LearnHub has established a subcontracted partnership with PillLab to provide specific training to PillLab employees.	LearnHub recently merged with another e-learning provider to expand its course offerings and marketing capabilities.

Company	Joint venture	Strategic alliance	Subcontracting partnership	Merger
WarAid	WarAid and AtlFish have formed a joint venture to provide logistics services for humanitarian missions in Africa.	WarAid and VIPBank have formed a strategic alliance to provide banking services to war veterans.	WarAid has established a subcontracted partnership with DeliFreez to provide food rations to war zones.	WarAid has recently merged with a non-governmental organisation to strengthen its impact and expand its reach.

6. Using cost-cutting strategies to improve the profitability of your business

By adopting cost reduction strategies, organisations can reduce expenses, increase operational efficiency and free up resources to invest in growth areas.

In a competitive market, it is essential for a company to remain agile and adapt quickly to change. Cost reduction strategies help capture this objective by optimising available resources, improving processes and maximising shareholder value.

For example, a manufacturing company may implement lean production methods to reduce waste, improve quality and increase productivity. Similarly, a service company may automate certain administrative processes to reduce labour costs and provide faster and better service to its customers.

The tracks to follow are:

- **Process streamlining**: inefficient and outdated processes can be a source of high costs for your company. It is important to streamline the processes to reduce production costs. By identifying inefficient processes, you can make changes to make them more efficient.

- **Outsourcing**: outsourcing non-critical processes can help your business reduce labour, infrastructure and equipment costs. You can outsource processes such as payroll, accounting, marketing, IT services and supply chain management.

- **Reducing procurement costs**: procurement costs can be considerable for businesses. By working with cheaper suppliers or negotiating long-term contracts, you can reduce your company's procurement costs.

- **Automation**: automating certain processes can help your business to reduce labour costs and increase efficiency. Automation can be employed for production, sales, and marketing procedures. This technology streamlines operational efficiency and reduces manual labour.

- **Use of technology**: the use of technology can help your company to reduce production, communication and marketing costs. Online collaboration tools, video conferencing and online project management can help your company reduce costs.

- **Reducing energy costs**: Energy costs can be a significant part of your company's operating costs. By adopting environmentally friendly practices and investing in energy-efficient technologies, you can reduce your company's energy costs.

Applying these strategies to our core list, this can result in the following concrete results:

Way forward	FunCoop	OrAlu	AtlFish	HighSeaCo
Streamlining of processes	Implementation of an automated inventory management system to optimise production	Analysis of production processes to identify inefficient steps and optimise them	Optimisation of the supply chain to reduce transport and storage costs	Analysis of fishing processes to reduce waste and increase yield
Outsourcing	Outsourcing of equipment maintenance to reduce infrastructure costs	Outsourcing supply chain management to reduce logistics costs	Outsourcing payroll management to reduce administrative costs	Outsourcing ship maintenance to reduce infrastructure costs
Reduction of procurement costs	Negotiating long-term contracts with suppliers to reduce procurement costs	Working with local suppliers to reduce transport costs	Use of negotiation to obtain better prices from suppliers	Use of negotiation to obtain better prices from suppliers
Automation	Use of robots for fruit harvesting	Use of automated machines for aluminium production	Automation of fish sorting to increase the efficiency	Automation of fishing to increase efficiency

Way forward	FunCoop	OrAlu	AtlFish	HighSeaCo
Use of technology	Using virtual reality to train employees	Use of video conferencing to reduce travel costs	Use of online collaboration tools to coordinate remote operations	Using virtual reality to train crews
Reduction of energy costs	Installation of solar panels to reduce energy costs	Installation of an energy recovery system to reduce energy costs	Using wind power to reduce energy costs	Use of energy-efficient equipment to reduce costs
Streamlining of processes	Development of more efficient production methods to reduce production costs	Using online project management to optimise production processes	Developing a more efficient supply chain to reduce costs	Using automation to increase production efficiency
Outsourcing	Outsourcing of accounting and payroll to reduce administrative costs	Outsourcing public relations management to reduce marketing costs	Outsourcing supply chain management to reduce costs	Outsourcing maintenance to reduce maintenance costs
Reduction of procurement costs	Search for cheaper suppliers to reduce procurement costs	Negotiating long-term contracts with suppliers to reduce costs	Quality assessment of suppliers to avoid additional costs related to returns of defective products	Development of supply partnerships to obtain preferential rates
Automation	Use of robots in production to reduce labour costs	Automation of production to reduce labour costs	Automating quality management to reduce labour costs	Logistics automation to reduce labour costs

Way forward	DeliFreez	LuxCars	PillLab	WoodCo
Use of technology	Use of project management software to optimise production processes	Use of augmented-reality technologies for advertising	Use of quality management software to optimise production processes	Use of state-of-the-art technology for production and maintenance
Reduction of energy costs	Use of renewable energy sources for production	Use of energy-efficient technologies for production	Use of advanced technologies to reduce energy costs	Use of alternative energy sources to reduce energy costs
Streamlining of processes	Creation of an online banking platform to optimise bank account management processes	Streamline shipping processes with a real-time tracking application	Optimising learning processes with an e-learning platform	Use of a project management solution to optimise fundraising and donation management processes
Outsourcing	Outsourcing HR management to a specialist company	Outsourcing of logistics to a transport service provider	Outsourcing of training management to a specialist company	Outsourcing of field operation management to a service provider
Reduction of procurement costs	Negotiating long-term supply contracts to reduce office supply costs	Use of cheaper suppliers for shipping operations	Reduced maintenance costs for computer servers by switching to a cloud-based solution	Negotiating long-term contracts for medical supplies to reduce procurement costs
Automation	Automation of customer credit checks to speed up the loan application process	Automation of data entry to improve the accuracy and speed of shipping processes	Using chatbots to improve online customer service	Automating data collection to improve fundraising efficiency

Way forward	DeliFreez	LuxCars	PillLab	WoodCo
Use of technology	Use of electronic signatures to accelerate lending processes	Use of augmented reality to assist in planning shipping routes	Use of video conferencing to facilitate remote collaboration	Use of blockchain technology to ensure the transparency and security of transactions
Reduction of energy costs	Use of LED lighting to reduce energy consumption in the bank's premises	Use of electric trucks to reduce fuel consumption for shipping operations	Using solar energy to power e-learning facilities	Use of energy-efficient lighting solutions for humanitarian field operations

8   RESPONDING TO MARKET CHANGES

1. Using economic change to create opportunities for your business

The world is constantly changing, and the company must seize this as an opportunity and adjust business activities accordingly to take advantage of it.

Take the example of the Industrial Revolution in Europe in the 18th century. During this period, companies could take advantage of the boom in demand for manufactured goods by adopting new technologies, automating their processes and expanding their geographical reach. For example, the British textile company Brintons took advantage of the growing demand for carpets by adopting innovative technologies and expanding its customer base.

Similarly, in the twentieth century, the Great Depression saw the rise of companies such as Disney and IBM. Disney could to exploit the need for entertainment by producing popular animated films such as Snow White and the Seven Dwarfs, while IBM seized the opportunity to provide more efficient IT solutions, helping companies coordinate their business in a manner that increased profitability.

Closer to home, during the financial crisis of 2008, a new generation of start-ups took advantage of the opportunities created by the economic changes. Companies like Airbnb and Uber emerged to provide innovative solutions for renting accommodation and transport, respectively.

In short, your company's ability to adapt to economic changes can help you seise opportunities, grow and prosper. Stay on top of economic trends, observe changing consumer needs, and be prepared to take bold steps to seise opportunities as they arise.

2. Using technological change to innovate and improve your business

The use of technological change has revolutionised many sectors throughout history, from the invention of the wheel to the creation of the internet. Companies that innovate and use cutting-edge technologies achieve great success; those that do not adapt, however, fall behind.

A very well-known historical example is the car industry. Henry Ford introduced the assembly line for mass production of the Ford T, which dramatically reduced production costs and allowed the company to sell cars at an affordable price to the considerable public. The technology of mass production made it possible to satisfy a growing demand and contributed to the growth of the automobile industry worldwide.

Another example is Amazon. In 1994, the company was founded as an online bookshop. It rapidly changed and became an e-commerce giant. By adopting cutting-edge technologies for inventory management, express delivery and personalisation of the shopping experience for customers, Amazon has been able to gain a competitive edge.

More recently, the COVID-19 pandemic has allowed some companies to grow rapidly. Health technology companies have grown exponentially due to the increased demand for telemedicine tools, PPE and identification tests. Companies that have been able to adapt quickly to meet these needs have prospered.

Companies that can innovate and adapt to technological change can stay ahead of their competitors and improve their profitability. However, it is crucial to note that the introduction of new technologies can require considerable investments of time and money.

Some ideas for our core list:

| Company | Ideas for technological change | | |
	1	2	3
FunCoop	drones for crop monitoring	artificial intelligence for weather prediction	blockchain for product traceability
OrAlu	remote sensing for mineral exploration	automation for worker safety	augmented reality for employee training
AtlFish	IoT sensors to monitor fish stocks	data analysis for forecasting fishing seasons	autonomous ship technology for oceanographic data collection
HighSeaCo	robotics for the maintenance of oil installations	artificial intelligence for oil production optimisation	virtual reality for training offshore workers

Company	Ideas for technological change		
	1	2	3
DeliFreez	robotics to improve production efficiency	artificial intelligence to optimise manufacturing processes	virtual reality for employee training
LuxCars	autonomous driving technology to improve road safety	augmented reality for the design of new car models	additive manufacturing to reduce production costs
PillLab	3D printing for the manufacture of personalised medicines	blockchain technology to ensure the traceability of medicines	virtual reality for the training of health professionals
WoodCo	3D scanning to improve design and production accuracy	augmented reality for training workers on construction sites	the Internet of Things to monitor machines and prevent breakdowns
VIPBank	a loyalty programme for the bank's regular customers, offering benefits such as discounts on bank charges, points redeemable for gifts or travel	integrating artificial intelligence for automated operations	implement chatbots for 24/7 customer support
ColiShip	Real-time tracking of shipments via a mobile application	optimise logistics with route planning algorithms	Personalise delivery notifications for an improved customer experience
LearnHub	e-learning platform with interactive courses	virtual reality for learning simulations	chatbots to answer learners' questions
WarAid	online platform for donations with flexible payment options	data analysis for better resource allocation	Augmented reality to raise awareness of humanitarian causes

3. Using policy changes to anticipate market trends

Political changes often have a major impact on market trends, as they can influence regulations, tax policies, trade and international relations.

By anticipating and adjusting to the various changes that occur, companies can identify opportunities and risks to their business to make informed decisions to remain competitive and successful in an ever-changing environment.

A country that adopts stricter environmental legislation can encourage energy companies to invest in clean and renewable technologies. In doing so, they can seize new market opportunities and position themselves as responsible and innovative players.

To manage this, here are some proposals to adopt:

- **Keep up to date with political news**: stay informed about laws and regulations that may affect your business. Companies aware of these changes can adapt and adjust their strategy to remain competitive. The following political news will allow you to participate in ongoing discussions and debates so that you can influence political decisions and public policies in your interest.

- **Analyse political agendas**: political agendas can influence business decisions, especially in areas such as taxation, environmental regulations, health and safety, import-export rules, etc. Therefore, conduct a thorough analysis of political agendas to anticipate future changes and adjust your strategy accordingly. Therefore, conducting a thorough analysis of political agendas to anticipate future changes and adjust your strategy accordingly can give you a competitive advantage. Additionally, you will avoid unpleasant and costly surprises, such as fines or penalties for non-compliance with rules or regulations.

- **Participate in political debates**: political debates can provide information on upcoming policies and new government measures. Participate in these debates to influence policy decisions in line with your interests. Businesses can speak out on issues such as regulation, taxation, subsidies and trade policies.

- **Collaborate with political actors**: political actors can influence decisions and laws that directly affect your business. Collaboration can help create beneficial partnerships for your business, such as government subsidies, tax breaks or public-private partnerships. By building trust with political actors, you can also help shape government policies and programmes that can positively affect your business. Working with political actors can be a key element in the long-term success of your business.

- **Assess the impact of policies**: political decisions can affect business, the economy and consumer trends. Therefore, assess the impact of these policies and adapt your strategy accordingly. This may mean adjusting business priorities, adapting production practices, or implementing new marketing strategies. Assess the impact of policies so that you can adapt more quickly to changes and anticipate future trends. Some policies can have a positive impact on profitability in the long term.

Companies that do not take account of these changes and do not adapt to them risk financial difficulties or even bankruptcy.

Keep in mind those companies that have overlooked the impact of political change:

- **Blockbuster**: the company overlooked the rise of video streaming and failed to anticipate policy changes related to copyright. As a result, it lost its leadership position in the film rental business and eventually went bankrupt.

- **Kodak**: Kodak missed the digital shift by not considering the emergence of digital photography and failed to anticipate political changes related to environmental regulations. This led to a decline in demand for Kodak products, and the company eventually went bankrupt.

- **Toys "R" Us**: the company overlooked the rise of online shopping and failed to anticipate policy changes related to safety standards for children's products. As a result, it lost the market share and eventually went bankrupt.

- The airline **Air Berlin went** bankrupt in 2017 after neglecting political changes in the aviation sector. The company underestimated the impact of EU policies on the market, such as environmental regulations and restrictions on state subsidies.

- **Lehman Brothers** bank failed in 2008 because of its lack of understanding of political changes in the financial market. The bank ignored US government regulatory policies, which could have protected it from the global financial crisis.

4. Using demographic changes to reach a wider audience

The world's population is constantly changing, and businesses must adapt to these changes to remain competitive. We will explore the distinct ways in which businesses can use demographic changes to reach a wider audience.

The first step in using demographic change is to understand it. Demographic changes include factors such as age, gender, ethnicity and geographical location. Grasp the influence these factors might have on your target audience.

For example, if a company is looking to reach a younger audience, it will need to use marketing channels such as social networks, which are popular with young people. If a company is looking to reach an older audience, it will need to use marketing channels such as television and newspapers, which are popular with older people.

Once you capture the demographic changes, you can use the demographic data to tailor your marketing. With your target audience being women between the ages of 25 and 34, you can use ads and marketing messages that speak directly to this demographic.

Demographic changes may also require businesses to adapt to remain competitive. If a business has traditionally targeted an older audience, it may face challenges if it does not adapt to the changing demographics.

A company may have to adapt by changing its marketing strategy, developing new products or services that appeal to a different age group. Technology can also be a powerful tool to reach a younger audience, or online advertising to attract a new audience.

For the most up-to-date information on demographic changes, follow the publications of various bodies, such as the National Institute for Statistics and Economic Studies (INSEE), Eurostat, governmental and non-governmental organisations. Marketing agencies and market research companies can conduct surveys to obtain data.

Use data mining and data visualisation software to facilitate the processing of vast amounts of information. Analysis tools such as these can make this job much easier. These tools allow you to extract relevant information and visualise it in the form of graphs and tables for better understanding.

5. Using environmental change to adapt your business for the future

Environmental changes, whether technological, social, economic, political or ecological, are having a major impact on the way businesses operate and prosper. To remain competitive and successful in the long term, companies must adapt to these changes and integrate them into their overall strategy.

By anticipating and adapting to the changing environment, organisations can seize new opportunities, minimise risks and ensure their sustainability.

Take the example of the energy transition to renewable energy sources. Energy companies that identify and invest in this trend can take advantage of the growing demand for sustainable solutions and position their company as an industry leader.

Here are some proposed solutions:

- **Assess your company's environmental impact**: Analyse the areas that have the greatest influence on the environment to put in place measures to reduce the negative impacts of your company's activities.

- **Develop sustainable products and services**: Encourage your customers to reduce their environmental footprint. For example, a clothing company may use environmentally friendly materials to make sustainable clothing.

- **Reduce greenhouse gas emissions**: To increase the energy efficiency of facilities, include the use of alternative energy sources and/or reduce business travel.

- **Adopt sustainable business practices**: Use recycled materials and implement a responsible purchasing policy for waste reduction.

- **Raise awareness among customers and partners**: Communicate the actions you have taken to reduce your environmental impact and encourage your customers to adopt similar practices.

Considering environmental changes is now a major challenge for companies. Here are examples of companies that have successfully adapted their business model to these changes and benefited from financial or image gain:

- The French company "La Poste" has deployed electric vehicles for its delivery rounds, thus reducing its environmental impact and savings on fuel costs.

- The UK supermarket chain Tesco has adopted a policy of reducing the packaging of its products, thereby helping reduce the amount of waste produced and improving its image with consumers.

- Scandinavian airline SAS has reduced fuel consumption by switching to a more modern, energy-efficient aircraft, thereby cutting operating costs.

On the other hand, here are two examples of companies that have neglected the environmental impact of their activity and lost market share:

- The German energy company RWE has long used coal to generate electricity, but faced strong opposition from environmental groups and consumers who preferred cleaner energy sources, causing its market share to fall.

- The French tyre company Michelin has been criticised for its waste management and high-energy consumption, which has led to a loss of consumer confidence and market share.

6. Using regulatory changes to improve your company's compliance

Government regulations are measures put in place to protect society, the environment, employees and consumers. They are often complex and constantly changing, which can be a challenge for companies to comply with existing conventions.

However, companies that anticipate and adapt to regulatory changes can improve compliance, reduce legal risks and improve their brand image. Indeed, a company that demonstrates its commitment to complying with government regulations can build trust with its customers and employees.

To use regulatory changes to improve your company's compliance, you can take the following steps:

- **Identify the regulations that apply to your business**: assess the laws and regulations in your industry to identify the legal requirements and regulations with which your business must comply.

- **Assess your company's compliance**: conduct a compliance assessment of your company to identify areas. If you fail to meet legal and regulatory requirements, there will be consequences

- **Establish policies and procedures**: establish policies and procedures to ensure your company's compliance. Employees should be informed of all policies and procedures. They must be clearly defined and documented.

- **Train employees**: train all employees in your company's compliance policies and procedures, including any regulatory changes. Make sure they understand them thoroughly.

- **Monitor and audit compliance**: establish monitoring and auditing processes to track your company's compliance with applicable regulations.

- **React to regulatory changes**: stay up to date on regulatory changes in your industry and quickly adapt your company's policies and procedures to comply with these changes.

9 TECHNOLOGICAL INNOVATION AND AUTOMATION

1. Using technology to improve the efficiency of your business

By automating manual and repetitive tasks, companies can save time and reduce costs. Online collaboration tools increase communication and teamwork, whereas project management software helps to plan and organise.

Technology can also help improve the quality of products and services by endorsing more accurate data analysis and introducing real-time monitoring and evaluation tools.

The use of data collection and analysis tools allows companies to identify consumer needs and preferences to tailor their offers and communications.

Technological advances give companies the opportunity to maintain their competitive position by adapting quickly to changing markets and anticipating future trends.

Companies that adopt new technologies tend to be more innovative and agile, which can give them a competitive advantage.

- **In the primary sector**, the use of drones to monitor crops and harvests has become a common practise. This technology allows farmers to obtain accurate aerial images and collect data in real time to optimise yields and reduce production costs. Similarly, the use of biotechnology to improve seeds and fertilisers is another innovation that allows agricultural businesses to increase production while reducing environmental impact.

- **In the secondary sector**, technological advances have enabled large-scale automation of production. Robots and CNC (computer numerical control) machines have replaced manual workers in many industries, enabling faster and a more accurate production while reducing labour costs. Companies can also use the Internet of Things (IoT) to inspect their machines and predict breakdowns, reducing costly downtime.

- **In the third sector**, information and communication technologies (ICT) have transformed the way businesses interact with their customers. Companies are implementing the use of chatbots and AI to provide customers with fast and efficient service, 24 hours a day, 7 days a week. This allows them to offer round-the-clock support without having to increase their labour costs. Companies can also use customer data to personalise their marketing and offer special deals and promotions in real time.

Some suggestions for our list of examples:

| Company | Ideas for improvement through technology | | |
	Idea 1	Idea 2	Idea 3
FunCoop	drones to monitor and optimise production	precision agriculture to improve crop management	artificial intelligence to predict demand trends and adjust production
OrAlu	sensors to monitor and optimise mining production	optical sorting technology to increase the purity of extracted minerals	Machine learning to optimise mine plans and improve worker safety
AtlFish	GPS technology to track the movements of fish schools and improve fishing	Internet of Things technology to monitor environmental conditions and improve supply chain management	data analysis to optimise fishing methods and reduce losses
HighSeaCo	Internet of Things technology to monitor offshore oil production	Machine learning to optimise oil extraction methods	Augmented reality technology to train workers to perform complex tasks safely
DeliFreez	artificial intelligence to optimise production and reduce costs	implementation of an intelligent production chain to reduce losses	implementation of a predictive maintenance system to minimise downtime
LuxCars	integration of augmented reality into the design process to accelerate the development of new models	implementation of an automated manufacturing system to reduce labour costs	the Internet of Things to improve vehicle quality and safety
PillLab	molecular modelling to accelerate drug discovery	implementation of continuous production to reduce downtime	blockchain to improve drug traceability

Company	Ideas for improvement through technology		
	Idea 1	Idea 2	Idea 3
WoodCo	virtual reality for the design and planning of construction projects	drones to monitor construction projects and improve efficiency	implementation of a collaborative project management system to improve communication and coordination
VIPBank	AI for risk analysis and fraud detection	blockchain technology for international money transfers	chatbots to improve customer service
ColiShip	RFID technology for parcel tracking	virtual reality to train employees in safety	automation to improve logistics operations
LearnHub	machine learning technology to customise curricula for students	augmented reality to make lessons more interactive	chatbots to help students answer their questions
WarAid	blockchain technology to make donations more transparent and traceable	social networks to collect donations and raise awareness	data analysis technology to identify areas of need and plan interventions

2. Using automation to improve your business processes

Automation is like a wind blowing through your business processes, eliminating tedious and redundant tasks to make room for more strategic activities. It saves time and efficiency by avoiding individual errors and improving the speed of execution.

The machines can take over complex tasks such as supply chain management, production and human resources management. By freeing employees from these time-consuming tasks, they can concentrate on more creative and value-added tasks.

Additionally, automation results in cost savings by eliminating the need for labour for repetitive tasks.

Here are some suggested solutions for using automation:

- **- Identify processes to automate**: Assess your company's most repetitive and time-consuming processes to determine which can benefit from automation.

- **- Evaluate the costs and benefits**: estimate the costs and benefits of automation to determine whether it is worthwhile for your business.

- **- Adopt the right technology**: choose a technology that will optimise the automation of processes. Ensure it is best suited for your needs. Many automation tools exist in the market, each with their own strengths and weaknesses.

- **- Train employees**: equip your employees with the necessary training on the latest technology and processes to ensure a smooth transition and gain maximum returns.

- **- Establish policies and procedures**: ensure the effective and consistent use of automation by establishing clear policies and procedures.

- **- Review and measure results**: track the results and performance of automated processes to identify areas for improvement and opportunities for optimisation.

- **- Continuously improve automated processes**: determine which areas could benefit from automation, and take steps to maximize efficiency.

3. Using data analysis to optimise your business performance

In today's business world, making informed decisions and optimising your company's performance is essential. This is where data analysis can play a key role.

Whether you are in the healthcare, financial or retail sector, this analysis will identify the trends, opportunities and challenges facing your business. With a thorough understanding of your data, you can consider more decisions that are informed and better position your business for success.

Let us look at the health sector in particular. Effective approaches to health data can reveal trends and problems, which in turn allows for creating programmes to prevent diseases and improve patient outcomes.

In the financial sector, this information will predict market trends and help investors make informed decisions. Machine learning algorithms use mathematical models to guide investors on which stocks to buy or sell.

In the retail sector, the company will understand the buying habits of their customers, and thus it will be easy to develop loyalty programmes, personalise offers and promotions, and ultimately improve the overall shopping experience.

Collect data reliably and ethically in accordance with the law, using the appropriate analysis tools to obtain meaningful results.

This is the approach to take:

- **- Data collection**: start by collecting data about your business, including sales, expenses, returns and customer feedback. Use data analysis tools to review this information and draw conclusions.

- **- Trend identification**: analyse data to identify trends in sales, customer preferences and spending. Use these trends to plan more effective sales and marketing strategies.

- **- Process optimisation**: find bottlenecks in your company's processes and optimise them to increase efficiency and reduce costs.

- **- Customer targeting**: identify the most profitable customer segments and target them to increase sales and profits.

- **- Improving customer satisfaction**: Collect customer issues or dissatisfaction and make changes to improve their experience.

- **- Measuring results**: regularly monitor the results of your efforts by using the data collected to evaluate the effectiveness of your strategies and adjust if necessary.

4. Using agile methods to improve the flexibility of your business

Agile methods are a project management approach that can help companies improve the flexibility of their business.

Agile approaches rely on iterative and incremental processes, which promote collaboration among different project teams. Teams work together to achieve specific goals within a given time frame. The focus is on delivering high-quality products or services, rather than on meeting deadlines.

Agile methods also allow for greater flexibility in project planning and execution, which can help companies adapt more quickly to change.

Software development has long benefited from this methodology; it is possible to use this approach successfully in other sectors. For example, a product manufacturing company can use agile methods to improve the flexibility of its supply chain by working with its suppliers to adapt quickly to fluctuations in market demand.

Similarly, a marketing company can apply this practise to adapt quickly to changes in market trends by working closely with its clients to understand their evolving needs.

To use agile methods effectively, companies must adopt a culture of collaboration and open communication. Team members must be encouraged to work together to achieve project goals, and leaders must be prepared to make decisions quickly to adapt to market changes.

Tools and technologies are also important for the successful implementation of agile methods. Online collaboration tools such as Slack, Asana and Trello can help team members communicate effectively and track project progress.

Advanced technologies such as the Internet of Things (IoT), data analytics and artificial intelligence are helping businesses adapt quickly to change by providing real-time market intelligence and trends.

Companies that adopt agile methods can be better equipped to remain competitive and thrive in an ever-changing business environment.

5. Using robotics to improve the quality and profitability of your business

Ah, robotics! The word conjures up images of futuristic, cutting-edge robots with almost limitless capabilities. However, the truth is that robotics is already widely used in many industries, and is increasingly available to small and medium-sized businesses.

Robotics can help companies improve their quality, efficiency and profitability. Automating repetitive tasks, observing and monitoring processes, and performing precision operations are just a few things robots can do. They have much greater potential, too.

Nevertheless, how can you use robotics to improve your business?

- **Automate repetitive tasks**: programmers can instruct robots to sort products, manipulate raw materials, and oversee machines that operate in a repetitive fashion. This frees workers from these tedious tasks, allowing them to focus on more vital and higher value-added tasks.

- **Improve accuracy**: robots are extremely accurate, making them ideal for tasks that require absolute precision, such as cutting, welding or screwing. Using robots for these tasks can reduce errors and improve the quality of finished products.

- **Examine and monitor processes**: robots can be equipped with sensors to observe production processes in real time, allowing problems to be identified quickly and action taken to resolve them. This can help reduce downtime and improve productivity.

- **Improving safety**: robots can accomplish hazardous or repetitive tasks, like managing delicate materials or keeping machinery in service. This reduces risks to workers and improves safety in the workplace.

It is true that the use of robotics may seem expensive for smaller companies. However, there are more and more affordable and convenient robotic solutions in the market. Companies can also start cautiously by using robots for specific tasks, before moving smoothly to broader automation.

As a reference, I propose three companies that have jumped on the market thanks to robotics:

- **Volkswagen AG** - The German car manufacturer has long used robots in its factories to improve production efficiency and car quality. The robots are used to weld, paint, assemble and inspect cars. By using robotics, Volkswagen has improved the quality of its cars while reducing production costs.

- **Nestlé** - Contrary to the advertisement with marmots, the famous Swiss food company uses robots for packaging and handling of products. The robots can work around the clock without interruption, allowing Nestlé to increase production capacity while maintaining consistent quality. By using robotics, Nestlé has been able to reduce its labour costs while improving the efficiency of its processes.

- **Fanuc** - This Japanese robotics company has been manufacturing robots for industrial automation for over 60 years. Fanuc robots are used in a wide variety of industries, including automotive, aerospace and electronics manufacturing. By using robotics, Fanuc has enabled its customers to reduce production costs, increase process efficiency and improve product quality.

Join the trend - explore the potential of robotics now!

6. Using AI to improve your company's business decisions

Artificial intelligence (AI) is transforming the business world, offering unprecedented opportunities for growth and innovation. By using AI, companies can improve decision-making, increase operational efficiency and enhance the customer experience.

One of the main uses of AI in the business world is data analysis. AI can process large amounts of data and identify trends and patterns that humans would be unable to detect. This can empower businesses to consider informed decisions based on data, rather than guesswork.

Another area where AI can be used is in business process optimisation. By using AI algorithms, companies can automate repetitive and time-consuming tasks, such as inventory management, production planning and supply chain management. This can not only reduce costs, but also improve the quality and speed of processes.

Additionally, AI can help enhance customers' experiences. Chatbots, for example, can answer customer questions quickly and efficiently, improving customer satisfaction. AI enables customisation of the customer experience. It uses data on customer preferences and behaviour to provide targeted offers and recommendations.

Finally, AI can help companies predict market trends and anticipate customer needs. By analysing social media data, sales data and customer data, companies can identify emerging trends and opportunities, which can give them a competitive advantage.

Companies that adopt AI can improve their profitability and competitiveness in the marketplace.

Be informed about the possibilities of AI to improve your business.

10   SECURITY AND PROTECTION OF THE COMPANY

1.   Using IT security to protect your business from online threats

As the world moves further into a digital era, companies must continually grapple with rising IT security risks. Cyberattacks can have disastrous consequences, ranging from data loss to disruption of business operations and corporate reputation.

IT security has thus become a major concern for all companies, regardless of their sector.

As cyber threats become more and more sophisticated, companies must act to secure their systems and data against these attacks. Detection may be difficult, but the risks are too great not to act.

Here are the main ways to improve IT security:

- **Education and training**: training employees on computer security practices is essential to prevent attacks. Train employees on the potential risks they might face and the security measures they should take. These include using strong passwords, closely checking suspicious emails, and being aware of phishing techniques.

- **Regular updates**: regular updates to software and operating systems can help prevent known security vulnerabilities. Organisations should make sure that they install the latest security patches on all their software. They should check for new updates regularly.

- **Network security**: secure your network, including using firewalls to restrict access to sensitive data, restricting user access to certain parts of the network and using intrusion detection tools to identify hacking attempts.

- **Regular data backup**: back up your data regularly so that you can recover it if it is lost or damaged. Companies can use online storage solutions or external hard drives to back up their data.

- **Access control**: Implement access control policies to limit access to sensitive data. This can include the use of strong passwords, two-factor authentication and limiting access to data based on roles and responsibilities.

Ultimately, IT security is an essential aspect of running a business. Companies must take steps to protect their systems and data from cyberattacks.

Often the manager neglects this part, but I will recall some very costly cases for the company.

- **JP Morgan Chase (2014)**: this bank suffered a data breach that affected over 76 million households and 7 million small businesses. The estimated loss was approximately $300 million.

- **Target (2013)**: this retail chain suffered a cyberattack that compromised the personal information of over 110 million customers. Around $300 million worth of losses were estimated.

- **Sony Pictures (2014)**: this company was the victim of a massive cyberattack that resulted in the disclosure of sensitive data and intellectual property. Approximately $100 million in losses were estimated.

- **Equifax (2017)**: this company suffered a data breach that exposed the personal information of over 143 million people. The estimate of the losses was $600 million.

- **Banque Rothschild (2008)**: this French private bank was the victim of a phishing attack that resulted in a loss of €2.1 million.

In each case, an effective IT security solution could have stemmed these considerable losses. Although the costs of these solutions seem high, they are minimal compared with the losses incurred in a data breach or cybercrime attack.

Companies must therefore invest in appropriate IT security to protect their assets and reputation.

Do not be next in line.

2. Using intellectual property to protect your business from competition

First, what is intellectual property? A set of legal rights protects intellectual creations, including inventions, trademarks, literary and artistic works, and trade secrets. Broadly speaking, these legal rights safeguard the intellectual outputs of individuals or organisations.

Why is this fundamental to your business? Well, if you have a unique invention or a distinctive trademark, you want to ensure that no one else can use it without your permission. This allows you to protect your investment and ensure that you have a competitive advantage over other companies in the market.

The most widespread forms of intellectual property include patents, trademarks, and copyrights.

- ➤ **Patents** are used to protect inventions and processes. If you have invented something new and useful, you can apply for a patent to ensure that no one else can copy or use it without your permission.

> **Trademarks are** used to protect brand names and logos. If you have created a distinctive brand for your business, you can protect it by registering it as a trademark.

> **Copyright is** used to protect literary and artistic works, such as books, songs and films. If you have created an original work, you can protect it by registering it as a copyright.

Now that you know what IP is and why it is important, how can you use it to protect your business?

Here are some tips:

- **Apply for a patent for any unique invention or process you have developed.** By filing a patent, you will ensure that your invention is protected and that only you have the right to authorise its use. This will give you an edge over your competitors.

- **Register a trademark for your brand name and logo.** This will protect your investment in your brand and ensure that no one can use it without your permission.

- **Register a copyright for any literary or artistic work you have created.** This will ensure that your work is protected and that no one can use it without your consent.

- **Keep your trade secrets safe.** Ensure your confidential business information, such as product formulas or marketing strategies; are kept secure by keeping it secret.

- **Watch over your intellectual property and act if it is infringed.** If you think someone is using your IP without permission, act to secure your rights and defend your business.

3. Using legal tactics to protect your business from lawsuits

Businesses can face litigation for various reasons, ranging from intellectual property disputes to disputes with disgruntled employees or customers. Companies must take strategic steps to protect themselves from the risk of legal action.

Here are some suggestions for legal tactics that may help:

- **Enforce a clear and documented policy:** A clear and documented policy can help avoid disputes by providing clear guidance on the expectations and obligations of each party. Ensure that your company establishes a policy for all critical aspects of business activity, including confidentiality, security of computer systems and prevention of harassment

- **Train your staff:** ignorance is not a legal excuse. Ensure that your employees understand company policies and how to implement them. Regular training can help reinforce the importance of these policies and good practices.

- **Hire a lawyer**: A lawyer can provide legal advice on your company's policies and procedures. He or she can also help draft contracts, non-disclosure agreements and other important legal documents.

- **Conduct background checks**: Before hiring employees or doing business with partners or suppliers, conduct background checks to ensure that they have no previous legal problems. This can help to minimise the risk of future lawsuits.

- **Have liability insurance**: Liability insurance can help cover the costs of defence and compensation in the event of a lawsuit. Make sure you understand the terms of your insurance policy and that you have adequate cover for your business.

Legal tactics can be an effective tool for minimising risk. Understanding your needs remains essential, so work with professionals to put in place appropriate legal protection strategies.

4. Using crisis management tactics to protect your business from disruption

Crisis management tactics are essential to support your business and ensure its continuity. Whether it is a natural disaster, financial scandal or technology failure, a proactive and well-planned approach can mean the difference between survival and failure for your organisation.

Due to the COVID-19 outbreak, many companies had to adjust rapidly to new regulations and challenging market conditions. Some companies that could overcome these challenges generally had effective crisis management plans in place and were able to pivot quickly to meet the new requirements.

With this in mind, it is crucial to learn how to use crisis management tactics to protect your business from disruption and ensure long-term resilience.

These situations require the application of crisis management tactics:

- **Crisis management planning**: Companies should identify the potential risks they may face and develop action plans to deal with them. Regularly update these plans and inform all employees of them to ensure they understand and can cooperate in a crisis.

- **Effective communication**: to quickly inform employees, customers, partners and other stakeholders of the situation and the actions to be taken, use social media, emergency alerts, emails and phone calls as channels for quick and effective communication.

- **Flexibility and adaptation**: this involves reallocating resources to meet increased demand or reducing production to cope with a disruption in the supply chain. Companies must also be prepared to adjust their business strategy to meet changing market needs.

- **Training and preparation**: your team receives thorough training to prepare them for any potential crises. They are equipped with the skills necessary to handle such situations effectively. This includes training in safety, crisis management and effective communication. Employees should also be encouraged to report any potential risks and provide ideas to improve the company's crisis preparedness.

- **Evaluation and learning**: after a crisis, companies must evaluate their response and learn from mistakes to improve their future preparedness. The evaluation should include identifying the strengths and weaknesses of the company's response, as well as opportunities for improvement. These lessons should be incorporated into future crisis management plans to ensure a more effective response in the future.

Appropriate crisis management is essential to ensure business continuity and survival.

5) Using physical security tactics to protect your business from damage

Protecting assets, both tangible and intangible, from physical damage is fundamental to any business.

Physical security tactics can help prevent and reduce the risk of loss due to crime, natural disasters or accidents.

We will explore some of the best practices in physical security to house your business.

Primarily, it is essential to put in place security systems such as surveillance cameras, alarms and high-security locks to protect your business from burglary and intrusion. Also, train your staff in physical security and provide them with the tools to report any suspicious behaviour or dangerous situations.

Next, you should ensure that your business has a disaster preparedness plan to deal with events such as fires, floods or storms. This may include putting in place specific safety measures such as fire extinguishers, fire alarms, flood protection and storm shelters.

The workplace is a crucial element that should not be underestimated. Provide employees with personal protective devices such as helmets, gloves, goggles and FFP2 masks. Give them ongoing training in workplace safety.

In short, you have to ensure that your business has adequate insurance to cover losses from physical damage. This can include public liability policies, property damage insurance and business interruption insurance.

11 ADAPTATION AND STRATEGIC ADJUSTMENTS

1. Adapting your business to market fluctuations

Market fluctuations are inevitable and can cause serious problems if a company does not know how to adapt.

- **The first step is to understand market trends**. Continuously monitor changes in consumer behaviour, technological innovations, competitive movements and economic trends. To accomplish this, companies can use competitive and market intelligence tools, consumer surveys and data analysis.

- **The second step is to identify the company's strengths**. Every company has its own strengths and weaknesses. It is conceivable for a company to better position itself to cope with market fluctuations by identifying its strengths. For example, a company that is particularly good at manufacturing high-quality products may focus on expanding that product line, rather than diversifying its product range.

- **The third step is to be creative**. Be prepared to experiment with new things, changes in product lines, quality improvements, design changes, new marketing strategies or price adjustments are possible.

- **The fourth step is to remain agile**. React quickly to market changes by remaining flexible. Flatter organisational structures allow for more instantaneous and flexible decision-making.

Finally, it is important not to be afraid to ask for help. Companies can benefit from the expertise of external consultants or specialist staff to help them adapt to market fluctuations.

2. Adjusting your strategy in response to economic changes

Economic fluctuations, whether they are recessions, expansions or legislative changes, can have a significant impact on the market and consumer behaviour. By anticipating and adapting to these changes, companies can better navigate these uncertain environments and exploit the opportunities that arise.

In 2008, during the financial crisis, many companies had to adjust their strategies to cope with reduced consumer spending and scarce financial resources. Some companies managed to adapt by reducing costs, diversifying their revenue streams or focussing on market segments less affected by the crisis.

Here are some suggestions on how to proceed:

- **Understand the economic environment**: monitor key economic indicators, such as interest rates, unemployment rates, inflation, consumer spending, etc., to anticipate future economic changes.

- **Reassess your strategy**: look at your long-term objectives and decide whether you need to adjust them. You may also need to alter your approach to marketing, pricing, distribution, financing, etc.

- **Cutting costs**: In difficult economic times, to maintain profitability, it will be necessary to cut costs. You can look at your current expenses and find ways to save money, such as reducing the size of your business, closing some branches or implementing a more aggressive sales strategy.

- **Diversify your activities**: this may include expanding into new markets, creating new products or services, or seeking new business opportunities.

- **Strengthen your relationship with customers**: in times of economic crisis, offer special promotions, discounts, satisfaction guarantees or loyalty programmes to encourage customers to buy from you rather than your competitors.

3. Adjusting your business to comply with changing regulations

Keeping up with regulations to maintain compliance of your products and services often avoids costly penalties. Regulations are often complex and can change rapidly, making it difficult to comply with the latest requirements.

- **Staying informed:** keep abreast of the latest regulations and upcoming changes. Monitor official publications, collaborate with compliance specialists and join industry organisations to track the latest trends. Stay up-to-date on developments in your field.

- **Assess the impact of regulations**: the impact of new regulations on your business and determine what is required to stay compliant. This may include changes in business practices, hiring additional staff, or updating IT systems.

- **Implement measures to comply with regulations**: put in place policies, procedures and processes that ensure compliance. This may include training for employees, implementing additional security measures, and conducting regular audits to ensure that the company is always in compliance.

- **Maintain a culture of compliance within the company:** understand the importance of following regulations and the impact their work has on the company's compliance. Considering these factors is essential. Maintain open communication with regulators to resolve any compliance issues quickly.

4. Adjusting your business to meet new technology trends

In an ever-changing world, new technological trends play a crucial role in the success and competitiveness of companies. Adapting and responding to these trends helps to maintain a competitive edge and seise new opportunities for growth.

Companies that adjust quickly to technological change can improve their operations, offer innovative products and services, and meet the changing expectations of their customers.

Take the example of the digital transformation that has affected almost every industry. Companies that have been quick to embrace digital technologies, such as artificial intelligence, cloud computing and the Internet of Things, have been able to optimise their processes, strengthen their online presence and present better experiences to customers.

Here are some suggestions for adjusting your business to the new technological trends:

- Keep up to **date with the** latest technological advances and emerging trends. You can use online information sources, attend industry events, or consult experts in the field.

- **Establish a culture of innovation**: encourage your team to be creative and suggest innovative ideas to respond to new technology trends. Encourage collaboration between different departments in the company to develop appropriate solutions.

- **Invest in training for your staff**: provide training for your employees to help them acquire the skills needed to use new technologies. This can help them better understand trends and find with innovative solutions.

- **Develop a digital transformation strategy**: find out which business processes in your company could benefit from new technologies, then make improvements where necessary. Then, develop a strategy to implement and integrate them into your business.

- **Partner with technology companies**: work with technology companies to develop innovative solutions and benefit from their expertise. This can help you accelerate the implementation of new technologies in your business.

New and evolving technology trends can offer exceptional opportunities for companies to improve efficiency and profitability to remain competitive in your industry.

5. Adjusting your business to reduce costs and improve profitability

In an uncertain economic environment, it is imperative that companies look at ways to optimise their operations to maintain their competitiveness in the marketplace. Reducing costs and improving profitability remain crucial objectives for the sustainability of a company.

Nevertheless, it is important to find a balance between saving money and the well-being of employees, as well as maintaining the quality of products or services.

- **Re-examine your processes and operations**: analyse your daily workflows to find ways to optimise your processes and reduce costs. Identify processes that are too time-consuming or costly and look for alternative solutions.

- **Use technology to automate tasks**: eliminate human error by accelerating processes and reducing staffing requirements. Automation is still an excellent way to reduce costs.

- **Outsource certain tasks**: You can outsource your accounting, payroll or even customer service. This option lowers your costs by not having to hire full-time employees.

- **Negotiate with your suppliers**: get the best prices and payment terms. If you represent a loyal customer, you can negotiate discounted prices or additional benefits.

- **Reduce energy costs**: look for ways to reduce energy costs, for example by improving the insulation of your buildings, using energy-saving light bulbs or choosing energy-saving equipment.

- **Make informed choices about investments**: expensive investments may seem like a brilliant idea in the short term, but it is worth considering the long-term costs. Look for alternative options, or consider whether you can wait to invest.

- **Encourage collaboration and creativity**: employees can come up with ideas that can help save money, so it is worth encouraging communication and creativity in your company.

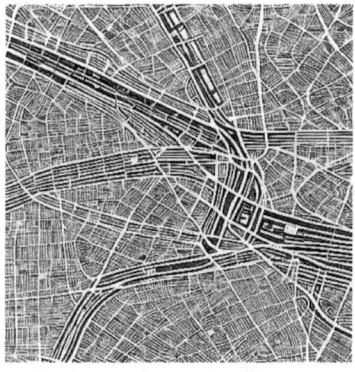

12   INFORMATION GATHERING AND COMPETITIVE INTELLIGENCE

1. Collecting competitive information in an ethical and legal manner

Gathering competition data in an appropriate and legally compliant manner requires a focus on publicly available information sources. Companies can conduct online searches of competitors' websites, review their annual reports and regulatory filings, and look at their social media activities.

Other sources of information may include market data published by third parties, industry publications and research reports.

Companies must take care to avoid spying and hacking when collecting information about their competitors. Such practices may be illegal and may damage the company's reputation.

Respect privacy laws and intellectual property rights, avoiding disclosure of sensitive information or infringement of competitors' patents, trademarks or copyrights.

2. Use the information collected to improve your business

This data allows you to identify opportunities, understand customer needs and adapt your offer accordingly.

By analysing and implementing the information gathered, you can make informed and strategic decisions to strengthen your company's position in the market.

An online retailer could use the data collected on its customers' buying behaviour to adjust its marketing strategies and optimise its offerings. By identifying the most popular products and customer preferences, the company could tailor its promotions and recommendations to maximise sales and customer satisfaction.

To make effective use of the information collected on the competition, here are some suggested solutions:

- **Perform a SWOT analysis** of your business against the competition. Examining the areas where you have a competitive advantage, as well as those in which you need improvement, will let you gain clear insight through this analysis.

- **Analyse your competitors' websites, social networking pages, advertisements, exclusive offers and promotions** to understand their marketing strategy. This will help you understand how they target their audience and how they position themselves in the market.

- **Analyse customer feedback on your competitors' products or services** to identify gaps and opportunities for improvement in your business. You can find these comments on social media platforms, online forums, product review sites, etc.

- **Attend industry events to meet competitors** and learn more about their business and strategy. This can also help you build relationships with other industry players who could be potential partners or customers.

- **Hire marketing consultants or research professionals** to conduct in-depth market research on your competition. This can include customer surveys, interviews with company representatives and data analysis to identify industry trends and opportunities for your business.

Use these different methods to collect competitive information ethically and legally, and then use this information to adapt to changes in the market.

3. **Use online monitoring tools to track competitor activity on social networks and websites**

Competition monitoring is important for several reasons.

First, it contributes to a better understanding of the market, facilitating the identification of trends, customer expectations and growth opportunities for informed decisions.

It then helps improve strategy by highlighting competitors' strengths and weaknesses, allowing you to adapt your approach accordingly. Additionally, it encourages innovation and differentiation, two key factors in absorbing and retaining customers.

These tools also simplify the benchmarking process, helping to identify areas of excellence and those requiring improvements.

Real-time monitoring helps spot opportunities and fend off threats quickly, ensuring that businesses remain flexible and responsive to market changes.

Here are some good practices to follow:

- **Identify competitors**: find the main players in the market with whom you are in direct competition so that you can concentrate your efforts on observing the right companies.

- **Choosing the appropriate tools**: There are many online monitoring tools available, each with different features. To monitor the activities of competitors, you can use tools such as :
  Hootsuite: a social media management platform that allows businesses and organisations to monitor, analyse and manage their social media activities
  Mention: allows brands and agencies to manage their digital presence through online monitoring and social networks.
  SEMrush: a marketing and advertising research platform that provides information on search strategies, keyword positioning and all kinds of web analysis
  Google Alerts: is a service that sends an email or alert when a new web page matching your chosen keywords appears in Google results

- **Define key performance indicators**: identify key performance indicators to monitor, including the number of followers on social platforms, website activity, search engine visibility and other relevant measures.

- **Analyse the results**: identify areas where you can improve your business with the information gathered. Implement the necessary changes to strengthen the problem area.

4. **Participate in industry events to learn more about the activities of the competition and to build relationships with potential partners**

You can attend conferences, trade shows and seminars to learn more about the latest industry trends and to meet opinion leaders and potential partners.

At these events, you have the opportunity to participate in workshops, roundtables and training sessions to learn more about the challenges and opportunities in your sector.

By meeting representatives of other companies, discuss their products and services, their business strategies and their achievements.

Participating in industry events helps to strengthen your online presence. Use hashtags and social media accounts to follow and participate in online discussions around the event. Post blog posts and status updates to share information about your company and to connect with other attendees.

5. **Use customer satisfaction surveys to obtain information on competitors' activities**

By asking questions about why customers have chosen your business over your competitors', you can understand what differentiates you from your competitors.

Ask questions about where your customers think your competitors are more effective than you, which can help you identify areas for improvement to be more competitive.

To maximise the effectiveness of your surveys, make them anonymous so that customers feel more comfortable giving their honest opinion. Provide rewards to encourage customers to respond.

Using this information, you can adjust your business strategy to better meet your customers' needs and remain competitive in the marketplace.

6. Using social media to monitor competitors' activities

Social media is now an essential tool for companies, not only to promote their products and services, but also to monitor the activities of their competitors.

Social media monitoring provides invaluable information about market trends, consumer preferences, and competitor strategies. This offers a chance to monitor customer reaction in real time and swiftly modify their strategy to exploit possibilities and avert risks.

For example, a cosmetics company can use social media to monitor the product launches of its competitors, as well as consumer reactions to these new products.

The company can investigate this information to spot the possibilities of creating new products or enhancing communication to fulfil the wishes and expectations of its customers more effectively.

Follow hashtags relevant to your industry to see what people are saying about competitors...and about you.

7. Using public information collection methods to understand the market

Public data remains a legal and reliable source if the data is recent.

There are several methods of collecting public information to integrate the market and better target customer needs.

Here are some examples of solutions that companies can use:

- **Online research**: find information on industry trends, consumer buying habits, customer feedback and competitive activity.

- **Focus groups**: gather information about customers' needs and preferences.

- **Surveys**: obtain valuable information about customers, such as product preferences, buying habits and satisfaction levels.

- **Data analysis**: gather information on consumer buying habits, industry trends and competitor performance.

- **- Industry publications**: follow industry trends and get information on competitors' strategies.

8. **Protect your company from competitive espionage by implementing appropriate security measures**

Competitive espionage can cause considerable damage to a company by revealing confidential information, such as product development plans, marketing strategies, customer lists and financial data, which can be used to the advantage of the competition.

Therefore, it is essential that companies put in place appropriate security measures to safeguard their sensitive information.

Do not neglect genuine security measures for several reasons. Primarily, spying on competitors is a common practice in many sectors, especially in the technology and defence sectors.

Moreover, companies that do not adopt adequate security measures are more likely to suffer financial losses and lose their competitive advantage.

Moreover, espionage has more legal implications. In many countries, competitive espionage is considered a criminal offence, and guilty companies can be held liable and face significant penalties.

Finally, implementing security measures can also enhance a company's reputation. Customers and business partners are more likely to trust a company that takes the security of its sensitive information seriously.

Here are some examples of negligence with serious consequences:

- **Coca-Cola**: In 2006, a former Coca-Cola employee was arrested for stealing confidential information, including product information and marketing strategies. The employer accused the employee of spying on competitors, and the employee accepted their guilt. Coca-Cola suffered considerable financial losses and a damaged reputation.

- **Google**: In 2010, Google was accused of violating the privacy of its users by collecting personal information on unsecured Wi-Fi networks. Many countries deemed this practice a violation of privacy law and ordered Google to pay hefty fines.

- **Uber**: In 2017, Uber admitted to hiding a data hack that had affected the personal information on 57 million of its users. This revelation led to government investigations and lawsuits, and Uber had to pay a $148 million fine to resolve the matter. The scandal significantly damaged the company's reputation.

To protect your business from competitive espionage, put appropriate security measures in place. Here are some steps to take:

- **Employee awareness**: Train your employees on information security and the risks of espionage. Make sure they are aware of common methods of attack, such as phishing and hacking.

- **Physical security**: restrict access to sensitive areas of your business, such as research and development labs, data centres and executive offices. Have security cameras to monitor entrances and exits.

- **IT security**: protect your business from hacking attacks and malware by using up-to-date security software and restricting access to sensitive data.

- **Intellectual property protection**: file patents to protect your inventions, and protect your trademarks by registering them.

- **Visitor control**: register visitors to your company in advance and provide them with a valid reason for being on the premises.

- **Communication monitoring**: use monitoring tools to monitor electronic communications, such as emails and instant messages.

ABOUT THE AUTHOR

The author of this guide is a recognised expert in the field of business management and IT. His strong academic background in IT and business management has given him a profound understanding of the challenges and opportunities facing modern organisations.

With 30 years of professional experience in the corporate world, the author has worked with companies of various sizes and sectors, helping them to optimise their processes and improve their profitability.

He has founded two successful companies during his career and continues to manage them, providing him with first-hand knowledge of the duties and difficulties that come with entrepreneurship.

Passionate about business and process optimisation, the author is constantly striving to share his knowledge and expertise with other professionals.

He believes that understanding the competitive landscape and adopting innovative strategies are essential to success in today's business world.

www.ingramcontent.com/pod-product-compliance
Lightning Source LLC
Chambersburg PA
CBHW080840220526
45467CB00008B/2346

* 9 7 9 8 3 8 8 6 6 4 1 4 3 *